RARITAN SKIFF BOOKS

EDITED BY

JACKSON LEARS

AND

KAREN PARKER LEARS

RARITAN SKIFF BOOKS
IS A COLLABORATION BETWEEN
RARITAN QUARTERLY
AND
RUTGERS UNIVERSITY PRESS

RARITAN
ON
WAR

AN ANTHOLOGY

◆

EDITED BY
JACKSON LEARS
AND
KAREN PARKER LEARS

RARITAN SKIFF BOOKS

PUBLISHED BY RUTGERS UNIVERSITY PRESS
New Brunswick, Camden, and Newark, New Jersey
London and Oxford

Rutgers University Press is a department of Rutgers, The State University of New Jersey, one of the leading public research universities in the nation. By publishing worldwide, it furthers the University's mission of dedication to excellence in teaching, scholarship, research, and clinical care.

Library of Congress Cataloging-in-Publication Data

Names: Lears, T. J. Jackson, 1947– editor. | Lears, Karen Parker, editor.
Title: Raritan on war : an anthology / edited by Jackson Lears
and Karen Parker Lears.
Other titles: Raritan.
Description: New Brunswick : Rutgers University Press,
2025. | "Raritan Skiff Books."
Identifiers: LCCN 2024018917 | ISBN 9781978841604 (paperback) |
ISBN 9781978841611 (hardcover) | ISBN 9781978841628 (epub) |
ISBN 9781978841635 (pdf)
Subjects: LCSH: War—Literary collections.
Classification: LCC PN6071.W35 R37 2025 |
DDC 808.8/0358—dc23/eng/20240718
LC record available at https://lccn.loc.gov/2024018917

A British Cataloging-in-Publication record for this book is available from the British Library.

This collection copyright © 2025 by Rutgers, The State University of New Jersey

Individual chapters copyright © 2025 in the names of their authors

All rights reserved

No part of this book may be reproduced or utilized in any form or by any means, electronic or mechanical, or by any information storage and retrieval system, without written permission from the publisher. Please contact Rutgers University Press, 106 Somerset Street, New Brunswick, NJ 08901. The only exception to this prohibition is "fair use" as defined by U.S. copyright law.

♾ The paper used in this publication meets the requirements of the American National Standard for Information Sciences—Permanence of Paper for Printed Library Materials, ANSI Z39.48-1992.

rutgersuniversitypress.org

CONTENTS

Introduction   vii

VICTORIA DE GRAZIA
You Are Not Alone, Stalingrad:
Reflections on the Seventy-Fifth Anniversary   3

PATRICK LAWRENCE
Assange behind Glass   32

MICHAEL MILLER
Six Years from Afghanistan (poetry)   58

C. FELIX AMERASINGHE
The Road to Revolution (fiction)   59

ANDREW J. BACEVICH
War and the Failures of the Fourth Estate   76

DAVID FERRY
A Translation from the Aeneid (poetry)   87

M. FORTUNA
Percussion of Cut and Salve (painting-assemblage)   90

PETER LaBIER
White Fright (painting)   92

RAY KLIMEK
Carbon Burn (digital chromogenic print)   94

d. mark levitt
god is water (painting)   96

CAI GUO-QIANG
Drawing for Transient Rainbow (drawing)   98

JOCHEN HELLBECK
and EMMA DODGE HANSON
Remembering Stalingrad (photo-essay)   101

ELIZABETH D. SAMET
Make Movies, Not War   115

KARL KIRCHWEY
Mutabor: Halberstadt (poetry)   140

ROBERT WESTBROOK
Bourne over Baghdad   156

LYLE JEREMY RUBIN
The Man Who Knew Too Much   170

TAMAS DOBOZY
The Animals of the Budapest Zoo, 1944–1945
(fiction)   177

SHEROD SANTOS
The Art of the Landscape (poetry)   191

Contributors   196

About the Editors   201

Image Credits   202

Permissions   203

Index   205

INTRODUCTION

War challenges the limits of language, confronting us constantly with its brutality, futility, and mendacity; descending ultimately into absurdity; sentencing us at last to silence—unless we take refuge in slogans. As Paul Fussell observed in *The Great War and Modern Memory*, a distrust of empty verbiage marked the inscriptions on the tombstones at the Somme, not the ones written by Rudyard Kipling, the solemn slogans, but the ones composed by the families of the dead themselves. "In addition to the still hopeful ones about dawn and fleeing shadows, we find some which are more 'modern,' that is, more personal, particular, and hopeless," Fussell writes, "and some read as if refusing to play the game of memorial language at all: 'a sorrow too deep for words.'" This vernacular modernism resurfaced in the minimalist vocabulary of ordinary American soldiers during World War II, so many of whom "just had a job to do" and "just didn't want to talk about it" when they returned home. This was more than inarticulateness in the face of the unimaginable; it was also an implicit recognition of the valor of silence.

Still the slogans survive in American public discourse, kept alive by politicians on their podiums and journalists at their keyboards, demanding military intervention abroad in the name of this abstract ideal or that anticipated crisis. The language of war ranges from the tired banalities of militarist rhetoric to the visceral combinations of horror, tenderness, and irony that mark the most memorable evocations of modern combat. Consider the scene in Joseph Heller's *Catch-22*, when the protagonist Yossarian goes to the rear of the plane to tend to the wounded gunner Snowden. Yossarian is relieved to discover that Snowden's wound is not as serious as he had thought at first. "'You're going to be all right, kid,'" he says. "'Everything's under control. . . . There, there.'" But then he notices Snowden gesturing downward with his chin. "Yossarian ripped open the snaps of Snowden's flak suit and heard himself scream wildly as Snowden's insides slithered down to the floor in a soggy pile and just kept dripping out." Yossarian "wondered how in the world to begin to save him." "'I'm cold,' Snowden whimpered, 'I'm cold.'" "'There, there,' Yossarian mumbled mechanically in a voice too low to be heard. 'There, there.'"

Even as he covers Snowden in the closest thing he can find to a shroud—the dying man's parachute—Yossarian continues to mumble the words a parent says to a frightened child: "There, there." It is a kind of incantation, an ontological reassurance: everything is still in its place; the cosmos is in order; it was only a bad dream. When his hope is smashed into fragments by his exposure to horror, Yossarian continues the reassurance, ritually, blindly: "There, there." This is tenderness in extremis, veering into absurdity, concluding in irony. Nothing is in its place; the cosmos is deranged; life—and death—are meaningless. Yet the impulse to affirm and express human connection survives, against all the odds.

Catch-22, like all the great literature of modern war, contrasts the carnage of everyday combat with the denatured idioms of military bureaucracy. Heller's Army Air Corps deploys a language system characterized by the absence of any evidentiary rules. Authority rather than referentiality determines the way events are represented. The representatives of authority create a grotesque linguistic atmosphere full of pseudo-strategic abstractions, such as the phrase "bomb pattern" that General Peckem keeps repeating in the hope it will enhance his prestige. By exposing such perversions of language, by laughing it to scorn, novelists like Heller and Kurt Vonnegut helped to explain (and implicitly to justify) the silence of the men who came back. For them this was the only sane response to unspeakable slaughter.

Yet even if, as Whitman said, "the real war will never get into the books," writers and artists keep trying to say the unsayable, in words and artifacts, sometimes with memorable results. We have assembled some remarkable examples of this work from the pages of

INTRODUCTION • ix

Raritan. Apart from the timeless *Aeneid*, every selection here casts light on modern war, observed or directly experienced, beginning with World War I. Most are grounded in particular places—as Ernest Hemingway wrote, "finally only the names of places had dignity"— Stalingrad, Halberstadt, Budapest, Baghdad, Algiers, the Tamil ghost towns of Sri Lanka, the six-by-twelve-foot cell in Belmarsh maximum security prison where Julian Assange was held for years without bail for the crime of revealing U.S. war crimes. Some recapture the actual experiences of war—the sight of a seven-year-old girl clutching her mother's hand, dodging explosions in the Halberstadt public square; the sound of a Mozart concerto in D minor, heard by a family hiding in a cave, played on their own piano by a Serbian sniper. Others take aim at the vast and vapid abstractions used to justify armed conflict, down to and including nuclear war.

Perhaps the most dangerous and duplicitous of those abstractions, at this historical moment, is the threadbare word "democracy." It has been ritually invoked in war-speech ever since Woodrow Wilson asked Congress for a war to make the world "safe for democracy." The great irony, as Randolph Bourne recognized at the time, is that the making of modern war undermines democracy at every turn, beginning with the demand for civilians' passive compliance with mass conscription, energizing the systematic efforts to spread war fever by infecting the populace with the big lies of propaganda, culminating in the huge apparatus of secrecy that conceals government decisions from public view. Secrecy is the mortal enemy of a well-informed citizenry. Without those citizens, democracy is an empty ritual. That is the strange atmosphere we inhabit today.

American secrecy came of age in 1947, with the refashioning of the U.S. government into the national security state. This involved the creation of the Central Intelligence Agency, whose remit included the systematic manufacture of "disinformation" (aka lies); it also included the renaming of the War Department as the "Department of Defense"—perhaps the foundational bureaucratic euphemism of recent American history. The Cold War nurtured a culture of secrets and lies that the population came to tolerate as a strategic necessity; the war on terror took that duplicity to new levels of sophistication. As the Downing Street memo revealed, the Bush administration had already decided to invade Iraq in the summer of 2002, and was shaping the intelligence reports alleging Saddam Hussein's weapons of mass destruction around the decision, rather than the decision around the intelligence.

The United States is now simultaneously engaged, overtly and covertly, in two overseas conflicts that threaten global conflagration. The first is the proxy war against Russia that uses Ukrainians as cannon fodder in a U.S.-led campaign to plant hostile NATO nations, some armed with nuclear weapons, along Russia's western border. The second is the Israeli campaign of mass murder and ethnic cleansing in Gaza, part of a larger strategy aimed at the erasure of any Palestinian presence from Greater Israel. American leaders, in seeking to justify their complicity in this carnage, have hammered a few more nails into democracy's coffin.

It is difficult if not impossible to find out what is happening in both Ukraine and Gaza, not only due to the inevitable "fog of war" but also to the U.S. government's suppression of inconvenient facts and dissenting voices. Censorship is especially challenging with respect to Gaza, given the breathtaking scale of Israeli war crimes— the haunting photographs of dead, maimed, and orphaned children; the piles of rubble concealing who knows how many dead or dying Palestinians. Yet the bipartisan support of both wars within the political class and the universal compliance of mainstream media with official dogma have ensured that antiwar sentiment remains largely invisible, however pervasive it might be in everyday American life. When dissent has surfaced, as in the dozens of pro-Palestinian encampments that appeared on college campuses this winter and spring, in nearly every case the official response has been swift and sure: call out the cops, in full riot gear, to disperse the protest. So much for the right of the people peaceably to assemble—what we once thought was a core democratic practice.

These are sad times for our country. "Democracy" has become one of those words like "sacred, glorious, and sacrifice" that Hemingway found at best embarrassing, at worst obscene, alongside piles of corpses. If the meaning of democracy can somehow be resurrected, it will have to be partly through honest critical engagement with the wars fought in its name. That is one hope animating this book.

Jackson Lears
Karen Parker Lears
Furman's Corner, New Jersey
July 2024

RARITAN
ON
WAR

You Are Not Alone, Stalingrad: Reflections on the Seventy-Fifth Anniversary
VICTORIA DE GRAZIA

for Arno J. Mayer

THE FIRST TIME I heard a tribute to Stalingrad in my American homeland was at the family Thanksgiving in 1991. Our guest, a young Soviet statistician, had just been seated when my father unexpectedly raised his glass to "thank all the brave Soviet soldiers." "If not for them," he said, "maybe I, or one of my brothers, would have been killed or wounded." The sight of Sergei in suburban New Jersey, arriving at the front door in his beaver ushanka and gray wool greatcoat looking battle frayed like many Soviet citizens in those times, had apparently jogged some memory.

It was back to Thanksgiving 1942 when my father, along with thousands of other young Americans about to deploy abroad, was anxiously following the great battle going on in Stalin's namesake city at the river bend on the lower Volga. At the time, the United States and Great Britain were still dickering about when to launch the famous second front to relieve the Red Army as it faced the Wehrmacht's seemingly unstoppable eastward surge. Meanwhile, the Soviet people bore the full brunt of Hitler's war. What a relief, then, when on 23 November the headlines trumpeted that the Red Army, after breaking the siege, had encircled Germany's Sixth Army in an invincible vise. The fighting would last ten more weeks before the last of the German forces surrendered on 2 February 1943. By then, the joint American-British forces had opened a second front against Hitler's Fortress Europe, moving across North Africa and up through Italy. The following May, my father, after being assigned to the cushy Psychological Warfare Unit at Camp Ritchie, Maryland, would embark for the Mediterranean theater to join in

4 • RARITAN ON WAR

the invasion of Sicily. Meanwhile, the war had turned. The Germans would never recover.

Nevertheless, the Soviets continued to bear the major brunt. At the time the Western Allies launched their first direct assault against the Third Reich on 6 June 1944 from the Normandy beachheads, most of Germany's 3.5 million military casualties had occurred on the Eastern Front. By the war's end, the Soviet Union was estimated to have suffered eight million military casualties and the loss of seventeen or eighteen million civilian lives. In the European theater, the United States suffered about two hundred thousand military casualties, and, of course, no civilian dead. Do the calculations: my father had good reason to be grateful.

After Sicily, he landed at Anzio, saw action at Monte Cassino, and occupied Rome, where he was put in command of Cinecittà. He was then redeployed to the south of France, liberated Dachau, and was photographed at Munich pushing Field Marshal Hermann Göring's fat behind into a military vehicle to take him off to prison. He came home after two and a half years with a slew of medals and ribbons, his service revolver, and snapshots of mounds of corpses, named his firstborn after his return Victoria, and often recalled the war as the best time of his life.

In 1991, I greatly appreciated my father's Thanksgiving toast. As a student in 1960s Europe, I had become deeply immersed in the culture of the old left, for whom Stalingrad, as the site of the *résistance à outrance* to Nazi fascism, remained the most vivid symbol. In his toast, I thought I heard him invoking the spirit of fraternal solidarity of the 1940s antifascist Popular Front.

But in retrospect, I wonder whether his gesture wasn't of a piece with the American way of war: favoring whenever possible the outsourcing of combat through proxies and alliances, heavy on matériel, technology, and sheer firepower, and cautious about expending its own manpower. This way of war making was driven in 1942 by the strong consensus about the rightness of the all-out war on Nazi fascism. And in that respect, the Battle of Stalingrad *was* the anti-

Axis military alliance's first important symbol. But this consensus was always undergirded by calculations that the war's costs to the nation in destruction and loss of life were practically nil in comparison to the giant leaps in terms of world power, prestige, and the existential validation from being on the side of good. In time, as alliances changed, scarcely any Americans recalled that the Battle of Stalingrad had once been regarded as not just the military but also the human and social face of the resistance to Nazi fascism's global conquest.

That loss is the prism through which I want to reflect on the Battle of Stalingrad, prompted by reading Jochen Hellbeck's *Stalingrad: The City That Defeated the Third Reich*, recently translated by Christopher Tauchen and Dominic Bonfiglio. Drawing on new archival sources, notably the interviews conducted over the course of the battle by the Russian Commission on the History of the Great Patriotic War, Hellbeck's book is at once an analysis and epic account on its own terms of the struggle between the two most formidable armies of World War II, each under orders to fight to the death. Reading Hellbeck moved me to reread Vasily Grossman's *Life and Fate* (completed in 1960 and first published in Switzerland in Russian in 1980), the one truly great novel inspired by World War II, which pivots around the battle; and, then, to go back to Nobel Prize winner Svetlana Alexievich's *The Unwomanly Face of War: An Oral History of Women in World War II* (1985), only recently rendered in readable English in Richard Pevear and Larissa Volokhonsky's new translation, to recall how she remembered Stalingrad. And there I found her mini-memoir of one indomitable veteran, who as a teenager, to volunteer for duty at Stalingrad, walked with a girlfriend the sixty kilometers of icy roads from their village with only one pair of boots between them; their only food was the lard sandwich her mother had prepared. Hellbeck's book also reminded me that whenever I teach the history of contemporary Europe, I have the class view Elem Klimov's *Come and See* (also from 1985), maybe the most significant cinematic reflection on the war

6 • RARITAN ON WAR

experience. We discuss why, even though they are inured to Holocaust imagery, the students are stunned at the atrocities committed by the German military against Byelorussian villagers (including their Jews). It is because they see them through the horrified eyes of a child partisan. And those eyes, it helps to know, were the director's own. Klimov had been born in Stalingrad, and nothing in his film, he said, exceeded the horror he felt as a child of ten, when, with his mother and baby brother, he was evacuated from the city in flames by raft over the burning slicks on the Volga.

◆   ◆   ◆

When Sergei flew back to Moscow on New Year's Day 1992, he traveled on a passport to a country that no longer existed. The Soviet Union had been dissolved. The Cold War was over. For European federalists, the hope was that this extraordinary turn of events would open the way for a Europe truly without borders, a prospect that had been decisively foreclosed when, at the onset of the Cold War, the Eurasian cape was split up into a Soviet-dominated Eastern bloc and an American-led Western one. According to this European federalist scenario, as the European Union extended eastward—and political democracy and free markets sped up the reforms started with glasnost and perestroika—the post-Soviet Russian Federation would eventually have joined it, together with the half-score of European states formerly under Soviet thrall. That was the brave hope going into the twenty-first century: that the new Europe originating out of the catastrophe of World War II would extend from the Ural Mountains to the Atlantic Coast.

Had that prospect come even close to being realized, united Europe's recently built memory palace would surely have welcomed a major retrospection on the Grand Alliance mounted in World War II to defeat the Axis. Such a retrospection would have taken stock of the annihilatory aims of the Nazi New Order's race war against the "Judeo-Bolshevik" Soviet Union, recognized that the attack on the USSR unleashed the genocide of the Jews, and acknowledged that the invasion accounted for a loss of life at least four times the numbers lost in the Holocaust of the European Jews (circa three million of whom were also Soviet citizens). It would have taken stock of the immense mobilization undertaken to defend against the Nazi invasion, which included the largest number of women ever to go to war, and its human and political costs. And it surely would have reopened the question of reparations. The wartime Allies had concurred at their final meeting at Potsdam in July–August 1945 that these reparations would be paid to the USSR for its incalculable losses, only to renege on the promise at the onset of the Cold War.

Finally, this retrospection, by foregrounding the remarkable meditation on the wartime experience in Soviet literature and film, would have substantially clarified the existential scope of the Axis war to remake the world, starting with the destruction of the Soviet Union. Understanding that experience would surely bring us closer not only to comprehending the nature of Germany's totalitarian war, and the individual and collective human and military struggle to defend against it, but also to grasping the political and psychic repercussions from the same war having been lived under such embarrassingly unequal terms in the United States and the USSR.

This rapprochement—and the retrospection—did not happen. As the United States emerged as the sole global superpower in the 1990s, the once formidable Soviet Armed Forces were dismantled, free-market experiments left the post-Soviet economy in shambles, and the European Union and NATO expanded eastward, but only to establish more and more distance between post-Soviet Russia and the West. Euro-optimists everywhere celebrated the newfound unity in the European Union as arising in reaction to the catastrophe of World War II and as a continuation, in some way, of the antifascist alliance. Yet the peoples who had sacrificed the most were as if missing in action. There was no hallowed shrine for the USSR's Great Patriotic War in the European Union's busy memory palace, no collective visits of German or French schoolchildren to Soviet

8 • RARITAN ON WAR

battle sites, nor hardly any exhibition space devoted to the Eastern Front in war museums. From what most Americans know about our alliances in World War II, you might believe that the Allied war against Hitler's New Order had at some point turned into the Allied war against totalitarianism, with Germany and the USSR switching sides, the former to become the pillar of the U.S.-led Atlantic Alliance and the latter, the Evil Empire, the mirror image of Hitler's Third Reich.

◆   ◆   ◆

To reflect on the human and political as well as the military significance of the Battle of Stalingrad on its seventy-fifth anniversary is a first act of historical reparation. That is the sense in which I want to reflect on Jochen Hellbeck's sober and humane *Stalingrad*. An expert on Russia in Soviet times, and noted for his use of oral history, Hellbeck pivots his history around a vivid collage of the three thousand or so interviews of civilians and combatants conducted by the Russian Commission on the History of the Great Patriotic War between December 1942, while the battle was in full force, and March 1943, when the battle had just been won and the roughly ninety thousand starving, frostbitten German prisoners of war, shivering in their filthy scorched and tattered greatcoats, were being shuffled off to concentration camps, nearly all to perish from cold, disease, and hunger. It testifies to the trust that Hellbeck enjoys among his Moscow informants that they originally alerted him to the whereabouts of the long-misplaced transcripts in a basement archive. It testifies to his own belief in the reparative effects of German-Russian scholarly collaboration that he joined colleagues at the Institute of Russian History of the Russian Academy of Sciences and at the German Historical Institute of Moscow to cull the thousands of pages of testimony from the original transcripts. It testifies, as well, to his deftness as an oral historian that he summons his long-dead interlocutors to speak to the most basic of questions about making war, which is why men—and women—fight.

This question seems especially weighty given that the six-month-long battle, lasting from August 1942 to February 1943, was symbolically, if not strategically, the most important military confrontation of World War II. It was also the bloodiest, if the civilian casualties are summed together with the military casualties. It is estimated that from 1.25 to 1.8 million people lost their lives, and the Battle of Stalingrad surpassed the casualty count of the year-long World War I Battle of Verdun, making it the single deadliest military engagement in history.

Hitler himself decided on the battle plan when he made the conquest of the onetime river-port town of Tsaritsyn—renamed for Stalin in 1925 in honor of his civil-war feats and swiftly transformed over the next decade into the region's largest industrial hub—a prerequisite to the Third Reich's final drive for control over western Eurasia. Having established Germany as the pivot point of a West European empire of allies, collaborators, and well-behaved neutral powers, in June 1941 Hitler reneged on his Non-Aggression Treaty with the USSR and invaded. The intention was to annihilate the USSR, subjugate its people, capture its resources, and populate it with Aryan settlements. After the Wehrmacht encircled entire Red Army divisions, took millions of prisoners, laid siege to Leningrad, and in October 1941 reached Moscow's outskirts, Hitler ordered the final push far south to capture the vital oil reserves on the Caspian Sea. In late July 1942, the Wehrmacht's Sixth Army moved against the heavily garrisoned city Stalingrad with its population of four hundred thousand swollen by one hundred fifty thousand or so refugees. By October, the German forces, after occupying half of the bombed-out city except for the sliver of riverbank along the Volga, launched their final offensive, only to meet unfathomably powerful resistance.

Stalin, in turn, made it a point of honor to recapture the city after his initial military flubs. Going on the offensive in November, the Red Army exploited the weaknesses of Hitler's command—namely, the Sixth Army had overextended its supply lines; its flanks were defended by Germany's much weaker and undersupplied

Hungarian, Italian, and Romanian coalition partners; and it lacked the equipment to carry on for long in the frigid weather. Once the Soviet counterattack had entrapped the German forces, Operation Winter Storm (the Wehrmacht counteroffensive mounted in December) failed to break them out, and Hitler refused to contemplate their withdrawal, the Sixth Army with its quarter of a million soldiers faced annihilation. On 8 January 1943, the Soviet command delivered an ultimatum to General Paulus to surrender with honor, only to have the Führer forbid it. It took another three weeks before Paulus (whom Hitler had meanwhile promoted to field marshal) was located in his command post in the basement of the Univermag department store, lying in a rag-covered bed, unshaven, and surrounded by waist-high piles of rubble, garbage, and excrement. His abject surrender (instead of committing suicide, as Hitler intended) ended the myth of German invincibility.

The Nazi leadership, in turn, exploited the shocking defeat to justify redoubling the Third Reich's war of racial extermination and to give voice to it officially for the first time. Reich propaganda minister Goebbels spoke for the Führer on 19 February 1943 when he blustered that Germany had hitherto underestimated "the true scale of the Jewish world revolution" behind "the Bolshevik War," whose aim was to "destroy the European continent." Henceforth, "no measure was too radical," "nothing was too ruthless" against "terrorist Jewry." From February 1943 on, the Final Solution to the Jewish Question gathered momentum, and the Axis war against the Soviets grew ever more implacable in its atrocities against civilians and prisoners of war.

At the same time, the Soviet resistance at Stalingrad relaunched the antifascist alliance globally. It redeemed Stalin from the disgrace of having signed the August 1939 Non-Aggression Pact with Germany and, jointly with Hitler, having invaded and partitioned Poland in September 1939. Stalingrad became the rallying cry for antifascist and anticapitalist armed movements from Mao Tse-tung's Red Army to the Italian, French, Yugoslav, Greek, and Vietnamese

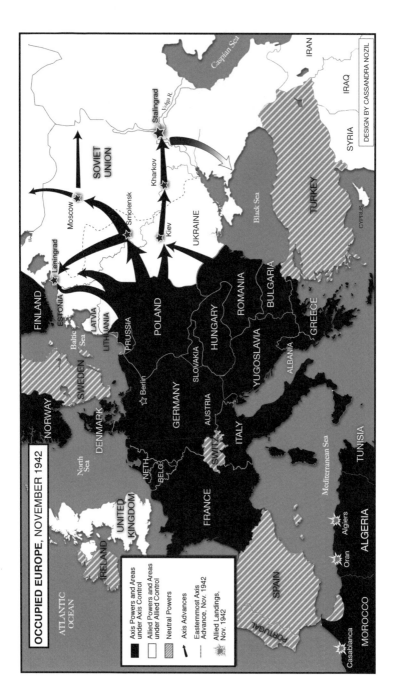

12 • RARITAN ON WAR

resistances. Postwar cities had squares, avenues, and streets renamed to honor Stalingrad. In Pablo Neruda, the city found its universal bard. He was in Mexico City, where he had found refuge following the antifascists' defeat in Spain, when he wrote "A Love Song to Stalingrad." It was September 1942, and Hitler's fascist army appeared on the cusp of another victory. Still writing in his hermetic style, he agonized, "Where are they, Your allies in a giant battle? / New York dancing . . . and London immersed / In a treacherous thought . . . Oh shame!" And when the battle turned, in "A New Love Song to Stalingrad," Neruda found a new voice as lyric poet of the world socialist movement, as he saw "life's sunrise / born with the sun of Stalingrad." He wrote, "Now fighting Americans, / white and dark like pomegranates, / kill the snake in the desert. / Ya no estás sola, Stalingrado . . . France returns to the barricades / You are not alone, Stalingrad."

◆   ◆   ◆

And the combatants, the people at the center of Hellbeck's history? In his didactic poem "The Worker Reads History," Bertolt Brecht, the other great bard of antifascism, asks, "Each page a victory. / At whose expense the victory ball?" Here, Hellbeck addresses that question from two premises. The first is that Stalingrad's defenders have to be credited with an astonishing military feat. Not only did they hold the city against overwhelming forces, but once the Germans were encircled, they fought on for three more months from building to building, hand to hand, to secure the capitulation of what were perhaps the best-equipped, most expertly disciplined, and most ideologically motivated troops ever mobilized for battle. The Soviet forces were also confronting the first invasion intended to eliminate or enslave the inhabitants of a fully populated modern industrial city. Starting in August, hundreds of low-flying planes bombarded at thirty-minute intervals around the clock; together with the incessantly firing mortar batteries, coordinated with flame-throwing heavy tank and infantry incursions, they killed thousands of civilians before most of the rest were evacuated. By September, the life expectancy of a newly arrived Soviet army private had dropped to less than twenty-four hours, and of an officer to seventy-two. To replenish this manpower, the Red Army, having exhausted its vast pools of White Russian workers and peasants, had to draw upon and give discipline to what officers had traditionally regarded as poor military material, meaning the raw peasant recruits from among the Soviet Empire's eight million or so male Uzbeks, Kazaks, Tartars, and Latvians, in addition to Soviet women, three million of whom were eventually conscripted for the war, 10 percent to serve in combat duty on one front or another.

Hellbeck's second premise is that Stalingrad's defenders have suffered not so much from being forgotten—there have been many books on Stalingrad, not to mention the innumerable online and video games about the battle—but from having been instrumentalized at every turn to make some larger, invariably tendentious or self-serving argument about the Russian people, the Soviet system, or Stalin.

The German invaders were only the first to be dismissive of the combatants. Once they got over their disbelief at the ferocity of the resistance, they marked the enemy, whom they already regarded as semi-Asiatic *Untermenschen*, as primitive, unfeeling brutes, motivated only by instinct and thus unaffected by the season or terrain, and who were thrown into counterattacks by commanders indifferent to human life. Because they seemed guileless, they were also dangerously deceitful. That the Soviets mobilized women and used them on the front lines, and that the women, too, fought to the death, only made them more contemptible.

Then there were the Soviet authorities, starting with Stalin, who, notwithstanding the immense effort to win the battle in his namesake city, refused to celebrate the collective feats of wartime once World War II was over. To defend the USSR, the Soviet people couldn't rest on their laurels. Paying tribute to the Red Army both detracted from doing honor to Stalin's omniscient war leadership

Soldiers from Rodimtsev's Guards division preparing an attack, September 1942.

and, with the onset of the Cold War, distracted from the new mobilization against the fascist West. When Stalin's successor, Nikita Khrushchev, relaunched commemorations of the Great Patriotic War, he approved plans for the enormous shrine on the Mamayev Kurgan heights overlooking Stalingrad, but only after the city had been renamed Volgograd to combat his predecessor's cult of personality. And when the giant complex opened in 1967—crowned by the statue of *The Motherland Calls*, which, at almost twice the height of the Statue of Liberty, eighty-five meters tall from her toes on the armored concrete plinth to the tip of her upraised steel sword, was the tallest female effigy ever built—it dwarfed the dead.

Western historians have been guilty of misrepresentation in another way, by treating Soviet soldiers as pawns of the Stalinist system, mobilized by the millions, thrown into futile battles, and prodded by political commissars, who, acting on Stalin's orders against retreat, forced them to choose between death from German machine-gun fire or execution at the hands of NKVD paramilitary detachments. "Ivan's War" was in every respect a no-win. If soldiers did express the conviction that they were part of the struggle to defend the Soviet Union from Nazi invaders, they were dupes of the totalitarian rhetoric of the times and of the monstrous Stalin, who would betray their every ideal at the return of peace.

Hellbeck keenly contests the latter contention—namely, that the combatants fought mainly under duress. Here, Stalin's mastery over making revolution and war mattered hugely. He mobilized the whole state and party—born out of the revolution, civil war, five-year plans, and the antikulak campaigns, purges, and cultural struggles of the 1930s—against the German invasion. As part of the patriotic revolutionary calls for struggle, he issued Order No. 270 in August 1941, which denounced any Red Army soldier captured alive as a traitor to the country. Said traitors' families could be deprived of military benefits and the wives of captured officers sent to labor camps. As the Wehrmacht launched its first assault against Stalingrad on 28 July 1942, Stalin issued Order No. 227: "Not One

16 • RARITAN ON WAR

Step Back!" The order commanded the military to hold the lines, keep workers in the factories to churn out war matériel, and bar any retreat across the Volga, the only way out of the bombarded, burning city. Hellbeck's witnesses testify that, to enforce the orders, NKVD squads were deployed to prevent the panicked flight of civilians and soldiers. Commanders boasted that they had ordered the executions of officers as well as of soldiers who fled, and the military detained at least forty-one thousand deserters. General Rodimtsev, the popular commander of the Thirteenth Guards Rifle Division, especially relished one platoon commander's handling of "bad soldiers": after he had sent out his scouts and sappers to prepare the assault against a German position, ordered his Uzbek troops to attack and seen them freeze under the withering German firepower, leaving his scouts and sappers to be killed, he "just lifted them up by their collars and shot them." Even if Hellbeck has found no evidence of mass executions, it is perfectly plausible that Red Army commanders shot refractory troops. In the trench warfare of World War I, it was common practice, and not only in autocratic Russia. It happened on occasion among the World War II Allied forces. And Stalin had hundreds of thousands executed for less.

Hellbeck's point here is, rather, that by October 1942, the resistance against the Germans had evolved into a people's war, the first ever to be fought in an industrial city. Faced with German military doctrine that operated combined-arms assault teams— close coordination between tanks, infantry, artillery, and air bombardment—the Soviet forces developed the strategic expedient of what Lieutenant General Chuikov of the Sixty-Second Army called "hugging the enemy." By keeping the front lines as close together as physically possible, they forced the Germans either to fight on their own or risk casualties from their supporting fire. Chuikov didn't mince words about how this strategy worked: "People think that urban warfare is a matter of walking down a street and shooting. That's nonsense. The streets are empty, and the fighting is going on in the buildings, in structures and courtyards where you've got to pluck the enemy out with bayonets and grenades." And with knives and spades and fists. "They face each other and flail at each other." The Germans, in turn, called it "Rat Warfare" (*Rattenskrieg*). They bitterly joked that, after struggling to take every street, factory, house, basement, and staircase, "even when they captured the kitchen they still had to fight for the living room." Chuikov's summation: "The Germans can't take it."

Fighting this way had to be highly motivated. Political commissars worked day and night to overcome their soldiers' fear and distress at dying—and killing. They circulated among the troops, giving lectures on the wartime situation, carrying agitprop suitcases with supplies of brochures and books, and promoting collective discussions of *Red Star*, the armed forces' daily. They distributed checkers and dominoes, and occasionally chocolate and citrus fruit, to raise morale. And they engaged soldiers in personal conversations, especially at night, as one commissar testified, when "the fighters are more inclined to speak openly, and one can crawl inside their souls." This attention surely raised morale enough to hold the lines: "Pull yourself back together, get ready to fight, and even if you're half dead, if you've only got one good arm, use it to shoot the enemy. Deal with that first one coming on the attack. Just deal with that first one. Your first shot will encourage your comrades."

More than that, the Communist Party military commissars introduced the Red Army to the same kinds of incentives that their peacetime counterparts, the factory commissars, had introduced to meet the production quotas of the five-year plans—namely, worker shock brigades, prizes, and incentives. The "new idea," as party bureau secretary A. F. Koshkarev of the 339th Rifle Regiment described it, was that "every soldier had to start a personal account of how many Germans he'd killed. . . . We would check these accounts, and if a comrade didn't have any dead Fritzes, we'd have talked with him, make him feel shame." The Red commissars named Heroes of the Day from among the troops and made their families proud by sending home their photographs and citations.

Fighting in Stalingrad's industrial district,
October 1942.

They awarded the Order of the Red Banner, the Order of the Red Star, and the coveted guards' status to battalions and whole divisions. Applying for the party card was more than a rite of passage; it promised to open the doors to a socialist heaven. Going into combat, Junior Sergeant A. S. Duka, Mortar Team, Second Battalion said, "The one thing I wanted to know was that if I died, I'd die a Bolshevik." Together with eight other men from his gun battery, he had applied on the eve of battle. Since getting the card was conditional on surviving, he went into battle "determined to prove himself." He survived. Two of his fellow candidates were killed.

◆ ◆ ◆

The really remarkable aspect of these testimonies is that they were recorded during the battle itself, and that they were intended to yield the documentary evidence for a work of world literature equal in stature to Leo Tolstoy's *War and Peace*. Isaak Mints, also called "the architect of Stalin's conception of the past," was the cultural impresa-

VICTORIA DE GRAZIA • 19

rio here. He was one of those uniquely Soviet academic-intellectual activists. An old-time Bolshevik, he had distinguished himself as a Red commissar during the civil war, so much so that the Communist Party, overcoming the bias against his Jewish-merchant roots that earlier had blocked him from attending Kharkov University, assigned him to complete his historical studies at the party's new Institute of Red Professors. From the early 1930s, he worked with the Soviet intellectual grandee Maxim Gorky to author the so-called *Collective Autobiography of the Soviet People during the Civil War*. Monumental in scope, and including scholarly analysis, documentary texts, memoirs, photographs, and artwork, this history by the people and for the people was intended to bear testimony "to the Human Being in capital letters, who showed others how to become more human than they already were." When the work finally came out in all of its fifteen volumes in 1935, it met the fate of other utopian projects intended to create Soviet culture's New Man and New Civilization: the political authorities pulped it practically immediately and many of its protagonists disappeared in Stalin's Great Purges. If Mints was daunted, as he must have been, having barely escaped himself, he rebounded at the opportunity to chronicle socialism's next epochal struggle, the Great Patriotic War. With full backing from the party, he arrived in Stalingrad in December 1942 to document the "joy, and grief, leisure and combat, home front and war front."

What is striking is how much affection the testimonials express for, say, the Tractor Factory or the Red October Steelworks, the sites of some of the cruelest fighting. Employing tens of thousands of workers, they were the pride of Soviet machine manufacture, and the hub of nearby mechanical workshops, engineering schools, medical centers, cafeterias, and housing that served many more thousands of people. Their principals stood in their rubble while they were being interviewed, ruthlessly factual about still standing in the main line of battle, yet wholly confident they would rebuild.

How much nuance of character emerges from ordinary men, tasked to perform horrible feats. The sniper Anatoly Chekhov

20 • RARITAN ON WAR

recalled how he shot his first German: "I felt terrible. I had killed a human being. But then I thought of our people—and I started to mercilessly fire on them. I've become a barbaric person, I kill them. I hate them." When he was interviewed, Chekhov had already killed forty Germans—most of them with a shot to the head. "One sees the young girls, the children, who hang from the trees in the park," said another renowned sniper, Vassily Zaytsev. This "has a tremendous impact," he added, alluding to the marauding German soldiery who, as they settled into life in the ruins, would at whim enslave, rape, pillage, and murder the civilians who had been left stranded after the evacuation.

The true hero here is the city itself. Hellbeck preserves the collective voice of the testimonials, adding to its chorality with interviews and diaries from German combatants, whose ordinariness as common soldiers—they were terrified at capture and desired only to get warm, eat a hot meal, and go home—make them no less hateful as invaders. Vasily Grossman shows up here, in his vest, as the well-known war correspondent attached to the *Red Star*. Later, in *Life and Fate*, he would describe the new city "born out of the flames." This had "its own layout of streets and squares, its own underground buildings, its own traffic laws, its own commerce, factories, and artisans, its own cemeteries, concerts, and drinking parties." For that phase of the war, it had emerged as the "world capital," "its inhabitants living their lives only more intensely, heroically, because the conditions were so extreme."

In *Life and Fate*, Grossman captured the fleeting quality of their fame. The city had been open to the coming and going of journalists, foreign correspondents, and photographers, including peerless reporters for the *Boston Globe*, *Herald Tribune*, and the *New York Times*. Almost all, while they were there, believed they were in the midst of a world-historical battle pitting the forces of crisis-shaken capitalism spearheaded by the Nazi fascists against the forces of rising communism spearheaded by the USSR, the homeland of socialism. Yet as Grossman brought his own immense work

After returning to Stalingrad, refugees sit on the ruins where their home once stood, March 1943.

22 • RARITAN ON WAR

to a close, he wrote that newspapers all over the world had barely reported the details of the German surrender before "Hitler, Roosevelt and Churchill were looking for new crisis points in the war. Stalin was tapping the table with his finger and asking if arrangements had been completed to transfer the troops from Stalingrad to other Fronts." As that happened, the city's occupants faced the depressing realization that the "capital of the war against the Fascists was now no more than the icy ruins of what had once been a provincial industrial city and port." The Stalingrad "full of generals, experts in street fighting, strategic maps, armaments and well-kept communications trenches" had ceased to exist. It "had begun a new existence, similar to that of present-day Athens or Rome. Historians, museum guides, teachers and eternally bored schoolchildren, though not yet visible, had become its new masters."

In actuality, preserving the memory of this people's war turned into a political minefield. Mints himself was uninterested in shaping his testimonials into the story of Soviet humanity waging war for its own purposes—from fear, out of hatred, for the love of comrades, to do right by their commanders and men, to survive, to go home. Mints wanted a grand narrative of the Great Patriotic Struggle, unfolding as one with the teleology of the Communist Party's long march toward world socialism. But that, too, was too radical a vision for postwar Stalinism. Mints's own career would be derailed in 1949 after Stalin's anticosmopolitan campaign targeted him as a prominent academic historian and Jew. Thereafter, the Historical Commissions offices were disbanded, and the thousands of pages of stenographic notes were boxed up and forgotten until they were recovered, transcribed, translated, and published under Hellbeck's supervision as *Die Stalingrad Protokolle* (*The Stalingrad Protocols*).

♦   ♦   ♦

We can't imagine Hellbeck's own act of retrospection without considering the Germany of the mid-1980s in which he began his university studies. Hellbeck's father had begun to pick up Russian in

1943 before being drafted into the Wehrmacht at age seventeen, only to be sent to the Eastern Front in early 1945 to fend off the fast-advancing Soviets. At his father's urging, Hellbeck chose to study Russian, which was an unusual choice for a West German student at the time. However, East-West relations were opening up on the civil-society level, if not on the level of the Cold War blocs. In the 1970s, Western Europe, the Federal Republic in the lead, had made overtures to the Soviet bloc, overriding American opposition. However, détente had ended with a new standoff over arms limitations, which had led the United States under Jimmy Carter to try to outmaneuver the Soviets by installing nuclear-armed cruise and Pershing missiles on European soil, and then, under Ronald Reagan in 1983, to advance the Star Wars initiative, with its fantasy of a total defense shield. The launching of this new Cold War brought anti–arms-race activists, pacifists, women's groups, and environmentalists to join forces across Europe in fear that if the two great powers pursued their "exterminist" strategies, they would unleash another, this time apocalyptic, nuclear war. In socialist, especially Soviet, culture, these fears prompted a huge burst of interest in thinking about the Great Patriotic War in a new key. *Life and Fate*, after being censored until long after Grossman died in 1964, was finally published in Switzerland in 1980, first in Russian, then in French, garnering huge attention. Alexievich's *The Unwomanly Face of War*, after coming out in book form in 1985, sold over two million copies before the USSR fell apart at the end of the decade. In sum, well before glasnost or "openness" became official doctrine under Mikhail Gorbachev in 1986, Soviet culture had begun the deepest, richest retrospection on the war anywhere.

Yet the heating up of the new Cold War ensured that this retrospection was contained. Ronald Reagan took the first step to building a practicably impassable memory wall when in 1984, in order to signal the United States' endeavor to firm up military support for the Atlantic Alliance in Europe (as well as to launch his campaign for reelection), he seized on the celebration of the fortieth

24 · RARITAN ON WAR

anniversary of the D-Day landing. Previously, the Allied invasion of Normandy, on 6 June 1944, had been only spottily celebrated. With the Channel at Pointe du Hoc as his backdrop, standing high and giving a smart salute before European and U.S. veterans and heads of state, Reagan paid tribute to the platoons of Rangers— "the boys of Pointe du Hoc"—as they pulled themselves up over the cliffs, as if they were cowboys rappelling up their lassos, to deliver Europe from savagery and evil. Of course, Germany was not present. But neither were the Soviets, except in Reagan's clichéd rhetoric, as he lamented that the Soviets had gone on to reoccupy some of the European countries that had been liberated, then recalled "the great losses also suffered by the Russian people— 20 million perished," only to exhort the Soviet leadership—if it truly "shared with the United States the goal of peace"—to "give up the ways of conquest."

In the coming year, however, Reagan reached out to the German Federal Republic to reinstate it symbolically as well as militarily within the Western alliance. Helmut Kohl, the conservative Christian Democratic chancellor, was determined to have Germany recognized as a "normal country." His government risked unpopularity by supporting placing U.S. cruise and Pershing missiles on the continent; and if it flexed its muscles in foreign affairs, say, in Eastern Europe, he didn't want to be labeled a rabid nationalist, nor have his people, most of whom were born after the Third Reich, be forever stigmatized for Nazi deeds. With that intent, Reagan agreed that upon the earliest occasion, meaning the upcoming G7 Conference at Bonn in early May 1985, the two statesmen would gather at a conveniently located war cemetery where they could jointly pay honor to their war dead. Unfortunately, the closest convenient cemetery, at the Rhineland town of Bitburg by the Luxembourg border, was not only the final resting place for Wehrmacht soldiers but also held the graves of Waffen SS troops. What a political gaffe the event turned into when it was revealed that, after being transferred from the Eastern Front where they had committed atrocities against Soviet civilians, the SS had committed similar reprisals against French citizens. The public was duly reminded that the two leaders were there to honor, not the SS, but the regular Wehrmacht troops. But it was well known by then, having been documented by German and other researchers, that the Third Reich's onslaught against the Soviet Union was conducted as a race and ideological war as well as a military operation, and that the Wehrmacht was equally involved in committing atrocities.

That discovery was already feeding into the furious public debate going on in the Federal Republic over Germany's collective guilt—which Kohl was tapping into for nationalist ends. Just a couple of weeks after the Bitburg blunder, Ernst Nolte, the eminent historian-philosopher, a conservative, published an opinion piece in the *Frankfurter Allgemeine Zeitung* titled "The Past Which Will Not Pass." So long as the Germans continued to obsess about their collective guilt, he argued, they would never be able to build a healthy national identity. To that end, the Nazi dictatorship had to be rethought as only one moment in a long history, arising in a century rife with horrific violence. The true source of horror lay in "Asiatic" deeds, meaning the Armenian genocide, the Soviet Revolution, and Stalin's purges. In that light, Hitler's Operation Barbarossa was a preventive war to block Bolshevik expansion westward. To go forward, Germans had to remember the great positives in their past: beautiful Weimar, the birthplace of Goethe and the First Republic, and stately Potsdam, home of the soldier-king Frederick William I and Frederick the Great, later the capital of the German Empire.

For Jürgen Habermas, West Germany's leading contemporary philosopher, a man of the left, Nolte's arguments were "specious NATO philosophy colored with German nationalism." After the Third Reich, he replied, the Germans, whenever they remembered Weimar and Potsdam, also had to remember Auschwitz.

For Hellbeck, Germans will have to remember both Auschwitz and Stalingrad. Fittingly, his own way to Stalingrad came via his father, who made him a gift of Vasily Grossman's *Life and Fate*.

26 • RARITAN ON WAR

Grossman's novel was the *War and Peace* that the Soviet intelligentsia had long awaited. Grossman placed the embattled city at the center. In the figure of Viktor Shtrum, the physicist-turned-writer, Grossman interwove his own story as he bore witness to the battle as a war correspondent, before moving westward with the Red Army to liberate Ukraine. He then passed through his hometown, Berdichev, from where his mother had been deported. Eventually, he reached Poland and Treblinka, where she had been murdered in the gas chambers. Writing the "ruthless truth" about war was Grossman's vindication of human life—"the occasion to look into individuals' heads, one full of dire forebodings, another singing, one trying to identify a bird on a tree—soldiers dreaming of girls' breasts, dogs, sausages and poetry." In fascism, he saw a concept that "operates only with vast aggregates," in total denial of "separate individuality, of the meaning of 'a man.' The battle against this de-humanization," Grossman believed, came down to "the struggle for life [which] lies in the individual, in his modest peculiarities and his right to these peculiarities." Out of the debris of Stalingrad, then, arose the most fierce and compelling account of the totalitarianism of war imposed upon individuals, complicated by the arbitrariness of the Soviet political system, and only alleviated by acts of individual human kindness.

♦ ♦ ♦

How to commemorate Stalingrad in today's world? Grossman once said of a nation that "the longer [its] history, the more wars, invasions, wanderings, and periods of captivity it has seen, the greater the diversity of its faces." Stalingrad is analogous, and the complexity of the memory politics it has already generated is practically boundless. Almost immediately, its memory became central to the myth of antifascism. But how was that myth nurtured, and how did it wane as the lodestar of the Popular Front, hand in hand with the waning of the other symbols of the old left? Stalingrad was central to the way the Axis thought about the finale of its struggle for the

New World Order: Milan, if Mussolini could have had his puerile last wish, would have been turned into a Stalingrad against the Allied invaders. Stalingrad was, of course, central to the memory of the war for any individual who fought there. That went for Alexievich's women orderlies, nurses, and female sharpshooters. Surely, that would hold equally in an utterly different key for the surviving relatives of the Uzbek "bad soldiers," collared by their platoon commander in 1943 and shot when they balked at dying for the Soviet homeland.

For most of the years since the collapse of the Soviet Union, the annual commemoration of the battle, held on 2 February, the day that Field Marshal Paulus surrendered, has been a lackluster affair. Year after year, the temperature hovering around twenty degrees Fahrenheit, officials trudge up the marble steps to the Mamayev Kurgan Memorial to lay wreaths and salute the dead. In a public reenactment where the Univermag department store once stood, Sixth Army commanders surrender to Red Army officers. The most popular event sees women traffic police outfitted in Soviet-era uniforms parading in tribute to their predecessors, who in 1942 directed military vehicles and supply chains toward the front line. A giant fireworks display closes the day. It did not change much that in 1993 Volgograd was granted permission to rename itself Stalingrad for the day of commemoration.

The year 2015 saw a real innovation when, on the occasion of the European Union's commemoration of the seventieth year since the end of World War II, Germany's foreign minister, Frank-Walter Steinmeier, visited Volgograd alongside his Russian counterpart. At the same time as he was paying homage to the dead at the Soviet war cemetery and laying a wreath at the Mamayev Kurgan memorial, President Putin received Chancellor Merkel at the Kremlin. This was a signal that, despite the sanctions that the European Union and the United States had imposed to protest Russia's annexation of Crimea in 2014, the Federal Republic was prepared to restore good relations. Assuming Russia showed good

The Motherland Calls, Mamayev Kurgan, Volgograd, May 2015.

faith, Merkel held out an olive branch. Germany admitted guilt to the atrocities committed against Soviet prisoners of war during World War II and was prepared to offer reparations.

Clearly, Chancellor Merkel's gesture was calculated to placate Russian nationalism. To retaliate against the sanctions, the nationalist bloc in the Duma (the Russian Federation's lower house) had mounted a task force to compile its World War II war losses and bill Germany for reparations. The final bill used the estimate of €600 billion in damages made immediately after the war, and added to that sum the calculation that, if Germany had paid Israel €60 billion for the murder of six million Jews during the Holocaust, and Germany killed twenty-seven million in the USSR (sixteen million of whom were peaceful civilians), then Germany owed reparations of no less than €3–4 trillion. And that was without calculating wasted human capital: if the present-day Russian population were reckoned at being 300–400 million, instead of its current 143 million, then reparations should be calculated for the notch of 200 or so million in the population, and Germany charged for paying out another trillion or so in compensation.

If the sums the German government paid out turned out to be derisory (about €2,500 each for the four thousand surviving prisoners of war), the words accompanying the gesture clearly spelled out Germany's responsibility for war crimes. While Steinmeier was at Stalingrad and Merkel at the Kremlin, the German president, Joachim Gauck, who under the German Constitution is responsible for gestures of contrition and magnanimity, visited the Soviet war cemetery near the Stalag 326 Senne camp, where three hundred thousand Soviet prisoners had been held between 1941 and 1945. In his address, Gauck recognized that half of the 5.3 million Soviet prisoners in German hands had perished, compared with only a couple of hundred thousand British and American prisoners of war. "They succumbed miserably to disease, they starved to death, they were murdered," Gauck admitted, and he added that "the mass murder of six million Jews overlay other crimes," and that "unlike in the West, the war in the East was planned from the very start by the Nazi regime as an ideological war, a war of 'extermination and eradication'" against peoples who were "defamed as inferior."

And in the United States? It would take a geopolitical earthquake to see an American president bounding up the two hundred marble steps of the Mamayev Kurgan monument alongside President Putin to lay a wreath before the dead. And it would amount to a symbolic act of war against the European Union unless the ceremony of repacification was conducted multilaterally with European Union and NATO representatives at his side.

In compensation, the Anglophone academic study of commemorative politics will surely turn its giant firepower on Stalingrad, to explode the national—and in the case of Stalingrad also the international—myths, much as it has shot down self-serving myths about the war in Japan, Italy, Germany, and France. Whether this endeavor could help to explode America's own almost universally accepted war myths is the question.

In that vein, I began this retrospection close to home by recalling, and now by reinterpreting, my father's Thanksgiving 1991 toast to "all the brave Soviet soldiers." Would it be too harsh to conclude that he, too, was instrumentalizing the dead of Stalingrad to relish his memory of having fought the good fight? Could it be that, subconsciously, he was also seeking to mollify Sergei, who in his ushanka with his great height and soft big mustache, looked like a Red commissar? After all, Captain A. J. de Grazia Jr., for all of his bluster about the good fight, was no different from millions of other Americans who valued the Soviet people as a wartime ally, only to recoil from them in horror once the Cold War started.

And what if Sergei, instead of simulating gratitude with his battle-worn smile, had sighed and said, quoting from Svetlana Alexievich's speech at her Nobel ceremony: "Suffering is our capital, our natural resource. Not oil or gas—but suffering. It is the only thing we are able to produce consistently." Or if, after the toast, at the risk of spoiling the Thanksgiving cheer, somebody had mused that the United States won every one of its twentieth-century wartime victories elsewhere and overwhelmingly at the expense of other peoples' lands and other peoples' dead. When will we reckon with that history honestly and systematically?

Winter 2018

Assange behind Glass
PATRICK LAWRENCE

OF ALL THE IMAGES of Julian Assange made public over the years, three are indelibly haunting, even if, as we look at them, their import comes to us subliminally. These pictures date to the spring and autumn of 2019, when the WikiLeaks founder was arrested and imprisoned in London as a British court considered an American extradition request. In all three, he is photographed behind a pane of glass, a little as if he were a sea creature in an aquarium—near yet beyond our reach. In all three, he is confined in a security van about to take him away from crowds of press people, supporters, and, we have to assume, some stray passersby.

These are pictures of departures, then. When we look at them we find ourselves among those gathered at the scene and left behind. On the other side of the glass, with its strange reflections and refracted light, Assange is framed for us. He is remote within the frame, as figures in portrait paintings are remote. Even as he leaves us, Assange is already gone.

There is a Reuters photograph taken on 11 April 2019, the day Assange was arrested. Plainclothes police officers have carried him, corpse-like, down the steps of the Ecuadoran Embassy in Knightsbridge. His hair is long and brushed back severely, and he wears an unruly beard. From the police van's window he offers a resolute stare. Handcuffed, he raises both forearms to manage a thumbs-up gesture. The checkered band of a London cop's cap is visible behind him.

In an Associated Press photograph dated 1 May, a police van is taking Assange from a court appearance back to Belmarsh, a maximum-security prison in southeast London. His hair is short and his beard trimmed. His stare again conveys resolve. Assange holds up his left hand and curls his fingers into a fist. To his left in the picture plane, the glass reflects the distorted image of a brick apartment block. To his right, the flash of a camera illuminates an icy steel door just behind him.

The third image is a still from a video recorded after Assange had appeared in Westminster Magistrates' Court on 21 October. He is in the window of a van that belongs to GEOAmey, a private company that provides "secure prisoner transportation and custody services." Behind him is a steel door similar to the one in the second photograph, again illuminated by the flash of a camera. Assange is clean-shaven, gazing into the middle distance somewhere just above his head. The resolute stare is gone. Assange has no sign for us—we on the other side of the windowpane—no thumbs-up, no clenched fist. Some new kind of silence—a totalized, internalized silence—has been added to the silence imposed on Assange at the time of his arrest.

These images span six months. To place them side by side is to detect in outline the story of a very eventful half year in the life of Julian Assange. They are to me like shards of a broken bowl. Holding fragments of pottery in one's hand, one imagines the unseen whole, the object that is no more. So it is with my prints of the Assange photographs. I spread them on my desk. I study them, one to the next to the next, then again the same. They seem to me tiny pieces of a shattered life, a life deprived, a life by turns taken away.

The story the images tell is Assange's but also ours, in some measure the story of the way we in the Western democracies (or postdemocracies) now live. In this way the three pictures are mirrors, held up to us that we see ourselves as we are.

◆ ◆ ◆

The story of Julian Assange's arrest in April 2019 begins in another April, this one nine years earlier. Assange's exceptional endurance aside, there is nothing to admire in this story, much to hold in contempt. It is a story of false charges, cynical fabrications, unscrupulous prosecutors and judges, incessant breaches of law. There is physical abuse and psychological torture. Sweden, Britain, and latterly Ecuador have all conspired to deliver Assange to the United States for the offense, as is often noted, of breaching official walls of secrecy to expose multiple crimes, corruptions, and cover-ups. Assange is not charged with lying or disinformation or calumny or libel or anything else of this sort. The crime is exposure, shining the light of day where it must not shine.

I have wondered while writing this essay whether Julian Assange will ever again see the sky but from a walled and concertina-wired prison yard. At writing, his hour draws near. The British verdict on the Justice Department's extradition request is due shortly. It is a foregone conclusion. There will almost certainly be an appeal. The prosecution's case and the court procedure are multiply flawed, but again almost certainly, it is a matter of time before Assange is put on a plane to face trial in a federal court in Virginia where such cases are typically heard and ruled upon. This verdict is another foregone conclusion. To describe these as show trials is perfectly responsible. And it is part of the argument here that we must be mindful of the history and connotations this freighted term bears.

To return to that earlier April: on 5 April 2010 WikiLeaks released "Collateral Murder," the swiftly infamous video of a U.S. Army helicopter crew's mid-2007 attack on unarmed civilians in Baghdad. Three months later came "Afghan War Diary," seventy-five thousand documents that devastated official accounts of America's post-2001 campaign in Afghanistan. These were two of the most damaging leaks in U.S. military history. For the first time in its brief life, WikiLeaks had penetrated deeply into the citadels of official secrecy. This was stunningly confirmed with the release of "Iraq War Logs" (nearly 392,000 Army field reports) in October 2010 and, a month later, the phased publication of "Cablegate," a collection of State Department email messages that now comes to more than three million.

All of these releases derived from Assange's work with Army intelligence analyst Chelsea Manning. They were a blunt challenge to the ever-advancing sequestration of power in our postdemocracies and—let us say this now—to practices of mis- and disinformation that have long been routine in institutional Washington and the capitals of allied nations.

The 2010 publications stunned the Obama administration and the national-security apparatus invisibly but formidably behind it. There is much to suggest, on the basis of what is known, that Washington soon prevailed upon cooperative allies to encumber Assange with all manner of criminal charges, however far-fetched, trivial, or unrelated to the work of WikiLeaks these may be. Stratfor, a Texas company that provides intelligence services to a variety of defense contractors and federal government departments, began issuing directives of this kind within weeks of the "Cablegate" releases. "Pile on," one of its advisories reads. "Move him from country to country to face various charges for the next 25 years." It was WikiLeaks, ironically enough, that revealed these communications in a 2012 release called "The Global Intelligence Files."

While teleologies cannot be countenanced, what Stratfor recommended—to official clients in Washington, we can cautiously assume—is a strikingly apt description of Assange's fraught odyssey during the nine years prior to his 2019 arrest. Shortly after the release of "Afghan War Logs," Swedish prosecutors alleged that Assange had raped two women while in Stockholm for a media conference. These allegations would haunt Assange for many years. We now know, thanks to an investigation by Nils Melzer, the UN's special rapporteur for torture, that the Swedish case rested on corrupted police reports and fabricated evidence. Not even the two women with whom Assange had consensual relations supported prosecuting Assange on rape charges. Assange volunteered a statement to the Swedish police after prosecutors leaked falsified accusations to a Stockholm tabloid. He waited five weeks to be

36 · RARITAN ON WAR

questioned, but Swedish authorities never brought him in. In autumn 2010 he decamped for London on his attorney's advice and with Stockholm's assent.

With the coordination of trapeze artists, Britain took over where Sweden had left off. British authorities arrested Assange two months after his arrival, citing a sudden Swedish request for his extradition. While released on bail, Assange took asylum at the Ecuadoran Embassy when Sweden declined to confirm that it would not reextradite him to the United States were he to return to Stockholm to cooperate with Swedish investigators, as Assange wished to do. In time, the Swedish case melted like ice cream in the sun. Prosecutors formally dropped their case on 19 November 2019. They had never charged Assange with any offense, and no allegation was ever substantiated, but they had done their work: by this time an obliging new government in Ecuador, acting at Washington's behest, had canceled Assange's asylum. He was arrested for violating the terms of his bail but was immediately faced with another extradition order—this one from the United States. Country to country, charge to charge: Sweden, Britain, and Ecuador acted, oddly enough, according to the design Stratfor had earlier proposed.

The Justice Department's initial request for Assange's extradition was unsealed the day he was carried out of the embassy. He was charged with a single count of conspiracy to compromise a government computer—this during his work with Manning—and faced a maximum sentence of five years. It seemed at the time an oddly modest case and an oddly modest penalty given the extreme animosity official Washington had nursed since Assange published the Manning documents in 2010. But more and much worse was shortly to come. On 23 May, six weeks after his arrest, a district court in Virginia unsealed indictments charging Assange with seventeen additional offenses—these filed under the 1917 Espionage Act. This was a precipitous escalation of the American case. Assange suddenly faced sentences of up to 175 years should he be extradited and found guilty of all eighteen charges now lodged against him.

* * *

"Like many young people, I wanted to be on the cutting edge of civilization. Where were things going? I wanted to be on this edge. In fact, I wanted to get in front of this edge of the development of civilization. Because the old people were not already there."

That is Julian Assange talking to Ai Weiwei in 2015. The noted Chinese artist had visited Assange three years into his asylum with the Ecuadorans. Their exchange is a contribution to *In Defense of Julian Assange*, a compendium of commentaries (edited by Tariq Ali and Margaret Kunstler) published a few months after Assange's arrest at the embassy. "If you could learn fast you could get in front of where civilization was going," Assange said the September day he and Ai conversed. "So I tried to do that, and I was pretty good at it."

Assange became pretty good at it at a young age. He was hacking into the email queues of Pentagon generals while still a teenager in Australia. He understood very early that to be on the front edge of civilization meant penetrating the walls of secrecy behind which our most essential institutions—of government, statecraft, intelligence, defense—set the course of an ever more globalized civilization.

Assange's thought was not his alone. By the time he was scoring his first hacking hits, it was plain that a "culture of secrecy"—Daniel Patrick Moynihan's phrase—had grown like kudzu all around us. In *Secrecy*, Moynihan's 1998 survey of the phenomenon, the late senator wrote of "secrecy centers" throughout the American government, of "the routinization of secrecy," of "concealment as a modus vivendi." Something called the Information Security Oversight Office (ISSO)—a secret in itself to most of us—each year totes up the number of secrets government bodies created during the previous twelve months. As Moynihan explained, in essence the ISSO counts the documents classified in a given year. These, too, seem to grow year to year like a Southern weed.

38 • RARITAN ON WAR

Assange's original contributions to the questions of secrecy and concealment are four. One, he recognized, without inhibition and without allegiance to any orthodoxy, that our political culture's infinitely elaborated structures of secrecy are, indeed, where civilization is going. At this point, it is commonly assumed among paying-attention people that a small proportion of what our government decides and does is visible to us. Two, Assange understood that these structures must be penetrated if authentic forms of democracy are to survive. Hence his thought as to where the edge of civilization lies. Three, Assange saw the vital, make-or-break responsibility of the press if the walls of secrecy are to be dismantled. Finally, he devised an extraordinarily innovative means to open up these structures—the national-security state and its numerous appendages—for the first time since this tentacled organism began to develop in the years after World War II.

Assange registered "WikiLeaks" as a domain name in Iceland on 4 October 2006. The site's early publications were small bore—a Somali rebel's assassination plots, the leaked emails of Sarah Palin, then a vice-presidential candidate—but its potential as a technology and a means to protect sources was immediately evident. In these early years, WikiLeaks was understood to promise something very new in journalism, a resource that could fundamentally alter relations between those practicing the craft and the powers they reported upon. Traditional media initially embraced WikiLeaks; governments cast a cold eye for the same reasons.

All of the major releases of 2010, WikiLeaks's breakout year, derived from the Assange–Manning connection. Their work was made of what reporters and sources do in countless such interactions daily: Manning gave a journalist a story and evidence to support it; Assange cultivated his source and published the story. No serious appraisal of their relationship can otherwise describe what they did. But it is this relationship that the Justice Department deems a criminal conspiracy. This was the charge in the indictment unsealed the day of Assange's arrest at the Ecuadoran Embassy.

It is not clear, even now, how many sets of documents Manning conveyed to WikiLeaks. In "Gitmo Files," published in April 2011, WikiLeaks lifted the lid on the Army's shockingly cavalier treatment of captives at Guantánamo Bay. On 24 June 2020, the Justice Department filed a superseding indictment against Assange, in which it alleges that Manning was also the source of these documents. In my view this is almost certainly so, but as WikiLeaks does not reveal its sources—Assange's most essential principle—the origin of "Gitmo Files" has never been established. However this may be, it was not until the *Guardian* and other newspapers began publishing parts of Edward Snowden's immense data trove, in the summer of 2013, that any breach of secrecy matched in magnitude the releases Manning had given Assange.

Manning and Assange paid, and paid swiftly, for their fruitful collaboration. Sweden and Britain soon had Assange careening through a hall of mirrors made of largely manufactured allegations. Manning was arrested a month after WikiLeaks released "Collateral Murder." She then faced the first of numerous charges and was sentenced to thirty-five years' imprisonment three years later. Manning's treatment while detained was not much different from what awaited Assange at Belmarsh: it was harsh and in breach of law. At the Quantico Marine Corps base, where Manning was initially held, she was deprived of sleep, confined to solitary for long periods in a windowless six-by-twelve-foot cell, and at times stripped to her underwear. Juan Méndez, at this time the UN's rapporteur for torture, described these and other conditions as "cruel, inhuman, and degrading." It is unusual and by definition cruel that Manning was subsequently imprisoned at Fort Leavenworth, a men's military prison, despite having announced just prior to her sentencing that she identified as a woman. By 2016, three years into her sentence, she had attempted suicide twice.

Three days before vacating the White House in January 2017, Barack Obama commuted all but four months of Chelsea Manning's remaining sentence—roughly twenty-eight years of it. Her freedom

40 • RARITAN ON WAR

was brief. In March 2019, she was rearrested on contempt charges after refusing to testify before a grand jury investigating Assange. Prosecutors knew Manning's story well enough: she could not have spoken more plainly when she was first arrested. She had submitted to extensive questioning, confessed, and pleaded guilty at her earlier trial. They needed one thing from her this second time around: they needed her to support their conspiracy case against Assange. Manning had earlier testified that she acted alone when she hacked government computer systems. Now they wanted some indication, however scant, that Assange had directed her. An incautious phrase would do. Manning gave them nothing. "I will not participate in a secret process that I morally object to," Manning stated, "particularly one that has historically been used to entrap and persecute activists for protected political speech."

Manning returned to prison, this time to the women's wing of a federal facility, on 8 March 2019. There she remained for a year, keeping the faith. On 11 March 2020 Manning made a third suicide attempt. A federal judge ordered her release the following day.

◆ ◆ ◆

Whistleblowing and the exposure of the officially hidden have long and honorable traditions, in America and elsewhere. As one would logically expect, challenges to our empires of secrecy have grown more frequent along with the grotesque expansion of these antidemocratic domains. This has proceeded in consonance with the elaboration of the national-security state, beginning with Truman's fateful directive in 1952—kept secret for decades afterward—to authorize the new National Security Agency (NSA). The imperium we now live within, we may fairly say, has from the first been a furtive, undeclared and unnamed, there-and-not-there undertaking—secrets comprising its walls. With the keepers of secrets, more or less inevitably, come the breakers of secrets.

There are some illustrious names among the leakers and whistleblowers of our recent past. Most people's lists begin with Daniel

Ellsberg, he who passed the Pentagon Papers to the *New York Times* in 1971. Mark Felt, a career FBI official, was the Deep Throat of the Watergate scandal, although his name was made public only in 2005. Let us not forget Samuel Provance, the Army intelligence officer who exposed abusive practices at Abu Ghraib prison in Iraq in 2004, along with the attempted cover-up that followed.

The list—any good list—must go on and on, too many exemplary figures to mention. Bill Binney, Kirk Wiebe, Ed Loomis, and Tom Drake were senior NSA officials when, in the early years of our century, they exposed the corruptions associated with the agency's now-infamous surveillance systems. These four had a curious ancestor worth noting. Herbert Yardley directed the Cipher Bureau when, in 1931, he exposed the first monitoring and surveillance practices of an early iteration of the NSA.

Julian Assange cannot properly be assigned a place on any such roll call. His work concerns whistleblowing, but he is a journalist and publisher with no whistles of his own to blow. Assange's bravery when confronted with questions of principle and integrity, and the magnitude of what he determined to do, are the match of anyone's in the truth-telling tradition. But we cannot tuck Assange neatly into any file. His fate sets him apart, just as the figure we now see behind glass is apart from us. There is an historical discontinuity, too. What has been done to Assange since his arrest and detention, how, and by whom, is to be understood only by way of the most disturbing precedents. Let us call this the colonization of Assange's being—every aspect of it—by legal authorities with (a paradox here) no legal authority to act toward Assange as they do.

◆   ◆   ◆

About a month after Assange was sent to Belmarsh, a prison Britain uses to detain foreign nationals suspected of terrorist activity, he wrote a letter to Gordon Dimmack, an activist (and self-fashioned journalist) who follows the Assange case. At the time, Assange and

42 • RARITAN ON WAR

his defense attorneys were trying to frame their case against the American extradition request. *In Defense of Julian Assange* includes part of this letter. Here is a brief passage:

I have been isolated from all ability to prepare to defend myself. . . . I am unbroken albeit literally surrounded by murderers. But the days when I could read and speak and organize to defend myself, my ideals and my people are over until I am free.

This letter is dated 13 May 2019. At a preliminary extradition hearing shortly afterward, Assange's attorneys stated that their client was too ill to appear in court, even via video from Belmarsh. On the same day, WikiLeaks announced that Assange had been moved to the prison's hospital wing. One of his defense attorneys said at this time that on meeting Assange "it was not possible to conduct a normal conversation with him." A day later, Nils Melzer, the UN's rapporteur for torture, made public his findings on examining Assange, not quite a month after his arrest, in the company of medical experts. These were the first indications that Assange was being mistreated at Belmarsh. Here is part of what Melzer wrote:

The evidence is overwhelming and clear. Mr. Assange has been deliberately exposed, for a period of several years, to progressively severe forms of cruel, inhuman, or degrading treatment or punishment, the cumulative effect of which can only be described as psychological torture.

Assange next appeared in public on 21 October 2019, the date of the third image considered earlier, when he attended another preliminary hearing at the Westminster Magistrates' Court. This was an important occasion. Craig Murray was among those in court that day. Murray, a Scot and a former Foreign Office diplomat, stands among Assange's most dedicated supporters. The day after the Westminster hearing, he published a lengthy piece on his website. It circulated widely—no surprise given its astonishing account of Assange's enfeebled appearance and the willful corruptions evident throughout the proceeding. I will quote Murray's report at length. His language, along with the images he conveys to us, merit our close attention:

> I was badly shocked by just how much weight my friend has lost, by the speed his hair has receded and by the appearance of premature and vastly accelerated ageing. He has a pronounced limp I have never seen before. Since his arrest he has lost over 15kg [33 lbs.] in weight.
>
> But his physical appearance was not as shocking as his mental deterioration. When asked to give his name and date of birth, he struggled visibly over several seconds to recall both. . . . It was a real struggle for him to articulate the words and focus his train of thought. . . . Julian exhibited exactly the symptoms of a torture victim brought blinking into the light, particularly in terms of disorientation, confusion, and the real struggle to assert free will through the fog of learned helplessness.

In his account of the court proceeding, Murray describes a perverse farrago of farce, travesty, and tragedy. This was railroaded injustice by any properly disinterested reckoning. Assange was confined in a glass enclosure the whole of the hearing—as he has been in all court appearances since. District Judge Vanessa Baraitser, the presiding magistrate, ruled against Assange on each of the points his lawyers raised. They requested additional time to prepare a defense, given that Belmarsh had deprived Assange of his records and restricted his meetings with attorneys. There would be no such extension. They argued that the extradition treaty between the United States and Britain does not apply because it excludes political offenses. There would be no consideration of the nature of Assange's alleged crimes. A court in Madrid was at this time

44 · RARITAN ON WAR

reviewing evidence that the Central Intelligence Agency (CIA), through a Spanish company called UC Global, had spied on Assange while he resided with the Ecuadorans. Since this included occasions when Assange was conferring with his attorneys, a finding of guilt would be sufficient to nullify the extradition order: Baraitser took no interest in this self-evidently significant case.

Five U.S. government officials sat at the back of the courtroom. Prosecutors, led by Queen's Counsel James Lewis, scurried to confer with them before responding to each point the defense raised. Baraitser then ruled according to the prosecution's preferences. Here is Murray:

> At this stage it was unclear why we were sitting through this farce. The US government was dictating its instructions to Lewis, who was relaying those instructions to Baraitser, who was ruling them as her legal decision. . . . No one could sit there and believe they were in any part of a genuine legal process or that Baraitser was giving a moment's consideration to the arguments of the defense. Her facial expressions on the few occasions she looked at the defense ranged from contempt through boredom to sarcasm. . . . It was very plain there was no genuine process of legal consideration. What we had was a naked demonstration of the power of the state, and a naked dictation of the proceedings by the Americans.

Toward the end of his report, Murray offered a few details as to Assange's circumstances at Belmarsh. These, too, should be of interest to us:

> He is kept in complete isolation 23 hours a day. He is permitted 45 minutes of exercise. If he has to be moved, they clear the corridors before he walks down them and they lock all cell doors to ensure he has no contact with any other prisoner outside the short and strictly supervised exercise period. . . .

That the most gross abuse could be so open and undisguised is still a shock.

There are, indeed, gross abuses galore in the fate of Julian Assange during this time—and since, certainly. These abuses have been by turns political, physical, psychological, and at last judicial. When preliminaries ended and formal extradition hearings began last February, Assange was again confined to an armored glass box—unable to sit with his attorneys, unable to communicate with them while witnesses were called, with no access to the defense's court papers, with no chance to speak—a muted spectator at his own hearing. When Assange's defense protested his preposterous confinement in a secure dock as if he were a dangerous criminal, Baraitser asserted (yet more preposterously) that Assange would have to post bail to be released from his glass confinement and sit with his lawyers. By this time, the court had psychiatric documents diagnosing Assange with clinical depression. "I believe the Hannibal Lecter-style confinement of Assange," Craig Murray (again present) wrote, "is a deliberate attempt to drive Julian to suicide." There is something extreme in this conjecture, at least to the ordinarily democratic sensibility, but it is less so when considered against all that Assange could reveal—not least the grotesque and consequential fraud of "Russiagate"—once he is on American soil with little left to lose.

To be honest, I do not know how shocked one should be that we are able to watch as the United States and Britain abuse their power precisely to abuse Assange openly and without disguise. While there was a remarkably prevalent news blackout in the months after Assange's arrest, British and American authorities draw no curtain over the sorts of events I describe. What are we, on the other side of the glass separating us from Assange, to make of this?

Vanessa Baraitser's ostentatious condescension toward Assange gives us a striking and suggestive detail in this connection. Prosecutors acting for the Crown but conferring in plain sight with

46 · RARITAN ON WAR

American officials, indifferent to all legal propriety, give us another. It is often said that those who detain and try Assange intend to make an example of him—a flesh-and-blood warning to others who may attempt entrance into the empires of secrecy America and its allies operate within. This is certainly so, but it is not the whole of the case. The rest of us, without ambitions to blow whistles or expose official wrongdoings, are also objects of the exercise. As Assange is disoriented, so are we to imagine ourselves. His confusion is intended to be our own. Baraitser condescends to us when she condescends to Assange and his attorneys. His struggle to assert free will is—but precisely—our struggle. In his learned helplessness—a psychiatric term coined by behaviorists to denote a coerced surrender to authority—we recognize our own. Assange's totalized silence: again, it is to be ours. To gather these thoughts as one, we are meant to watch as the sovereign state demonstrates what the Assange case requires us to call limitless subordination. This phenomenon should not escape us.

"The arrest of Assange is scandalous in several respects," Noam Chomsky writes in his contribution to *In Defense of Julian Assange*. "One of them is just the show of government power." The linguist's words are deceptively freighted for all their apparent simplicity. In them lies the irreducible meaning of Julian Assange's fate. It is a question of purposeful display. What has become of power in the remnants of our democracies, the extent of its reach, what it guards at all costs, what it further aspires to, our relation to it: this is what we are meant to see.

◆　◆　◆

The Origins of Totalitarianism is commonly read as a condemnation of the Nazi and Stalinist regimes, specifically as these found their most debased expression in concentration and extermination camps. This is fine but insufficient. We cannot underestimate the pertinence to our circumstances of Hannah Arendt's tour-de-force exploration of what she termed "total domination." It is no good taking the camps or the systems that begot them as one-off aberrations to be excised from our understanding of history. This was Arendt's very point in giving us an account of totalitarianism that reaches back to the nineteenth century. She persuasively establishes the phenomenon as part of the modern condition, and I do not know that we have left off being modern.

Arendt runs relentlessly and deep as she defines total domination in its fulsome specificities. Its intent is to strip humanity of all identity and individuation. It is to reduce all who are subjected to it to an interchangeable "bundle of reactions," none in the slightest different from any other. Perfect predictability leads to perfect control. Here is Arendt on the means by which this is to be accomplished:

> Totalitarian domination attempts to achieve this through ideological indoctrination of the elite formations and through absolute terror in the camps. . . . The camps are meant not only to exterminate people and degrade human beings but also serve the ghastly experiment of eliminating, under scientifically controlled conditions, spontaneity itself as an expression of human behavior and of transforming the human personality into a mere thing. . . . So the experiment of total domination in the concentration camps depends on sealing off the latter against the world of all others, the world of the living in general.

We will come to our indoctrinated elites shortly. For now, let us remain with Arendt's thought of absolute terror. How far must we travel from her idea to the learned helplessness Craig Murray detected when he saw Assange in the Westminster court for the first time since his incarceration at Belmarsh? How shall we understand the Assange in our three images, the Assange rendered barely articulate over his months at Belmarsh, as we watch Arendt's acute mind at work? Certainly he has been sealed off against the world of all others. Do we witness—by glimpses, of course, our shards of pottery—a systematic effort to squeeze all spontaneity from him?

48 · RARITAN ON WAR

These questions are not difficult. Our replies require us merely to set aside the grim images of the camps we carry in our heads like frames in a grainy newsreel. Then, our minds clear, we must allow ourselves to think about convergences. History is our merciless but best guide. One of its bitterest lessons is the tendency of great powers to become what they stand against. The purportedly innocent are over time transformed into the guilty. The enemy of torture lapses into torture. The anti-imperial power becomes an empire. Hardly is the thought novel. It proves out almost invariably.

"What is a camp, what is its juridico-political structure?" the philosopher Giorgio Agamben asks in *Homo Sacer*, a brief book he subtitles *Sovereign Power and Bare Life*. "This will lead us to regard the camp not as historical fact and an anomaly belonging to the past (even if still verifiable) but in some way as the hidden matrix of the political space in which we are still living."

This is altogether bold on the Italian philosopher's part. But as we shed our resistance to so startling a thought, we read more clearly into what has become of Assange since his arrest. We can now recognize the purposeful extreme of his isolation—in prison but also from us, "the world of the living." No access to a computer, to his records, to (most of the time) a telephone: What is this if not an effort to obliterate identity to the extent possible, to strip away all spontaneity—which I take to mean autonomy, agency? What do we make of a man who struggles to say his name? In his helplessness do we see the previously robust doer of deeds reduced to a bundle of reactions?

Arendt does not seem to have explored how her discoveries might bear upon us now, we the living. But it is hardly too large a leap to think of Assange's time at Belmarsh—such as we know of it—as an experiment of the kind Arendt so well investigated. At its sordid core, there is the same effort to dismantle the personality. It is this Assange wrote of when he told Gordon Dimmack he was unbroken but surrounded by murderers—murderers of the spirit as well as those around him charged with homicide, in my reading of his letter. From the first of the photographs considered earlier to the person Craig Murray saw standing before Judge Baraitser six months later, we have a record of his tragic regress toward the condition of "mere thing." Borrowing from a scholar named Jon Pahl, let us call this "innocent domination"—the dominating power's claim to virtue in its act of domination.

Since Assange's first moments in captivity, when a half dozen police officers carried him down the Ecuadoran Embassy's steps, the corporeal dimension of the state's conduct has been very plain. This we must also consider. If the project is total domination, it must begin with the body. It is through the body that the prisoner is deprived of all control. Guantánamo Bay, Abu Ghraib, the CIA's secret torture sites, Chelsea Manning at Quantico and Leavenworth: there are many such cases, these merely the most readily to hand. The excessive use of prolonged solitary confinement at "supermax" prisons across the United States constitutes another. Bodily domination as a coldly efficient means of dehumanization, of assault on all constituents of identity: from the time of the camps until today, it is always in evidence. This is what we look at when we look through the glass at Assange.

It would be illusory to posit that this use of the body is something new in the Western democracies. Slavery, the American Indian campaigns, the World War II internment camps: these are obvious precedents. But in this contemporary iteration we nonetheless find an unprecedented descent into convergences with some of the most detested features of the West's twentieth-century totalitarian adversaries. Routinized torture, the pervasive reach of surveillance into the spaces of daily life, lately the systematic punishment of innocent populations by means of diabolically calibrated sanctions, and now what amounts to the physical and mental abduction of those challenging the vast universes of sovereign secrets—all of this must concern us partly as a matter of morality but also because we are subject to it ourselves. We watch as our sovereign institutions, one after another, destroy themselves with illegitimate assertions of sovereignty. While once we looked to them for protection, we—we, all of us—must now seek protection from them. This is the lesson Assange in captivity has for us.

Nowhere is this of graver consequence than in the case of our judiciaries. It is when judicial systems lapse that a society's final fate becomes evident. Judges and courts are the last line of defense against "failing state" status. We must consider Vanessa Baraitser's imperious performance in this context. With her flagrant corruptions of due process and her high-handed demeanor, what is it she sought to convey, seated as she was in an English judge's robe and peruke?

The relationship between law and lawgiver has preoccupied many a political philosopher over many centuries. In the modern West, where the citizenry is declared sovereign, those who make law and enforce law are assumed to be bound by law. It is difficult to think of Baraitser as a Cicero-reading legal scholar, but she nonetheless took a strong position as to the purview of law. By word, gesture, and deed, she placed the giver of law outside the law. Those who consider this question in our time, Arendt and Agamben among them, define this as a "state of exception." Sovereign power declares itself the exception to its own laws. This leaves the state inside and outside the judicial order at the same time, for it cannot be an exception unless there is a judicial order from which it is excepted. The sovereign extends law over the governed, in other words, so as to demonstrate its position above it. Agamben expresses the paradox this way: "I, the sovereign, who am outside the law, declare that there is nothing outside the law." This is Baraitser's implicit but very clear position: I, Judge Baraitser, embody the law and enforce it. I am not bound by the law I uphold.

"Everything is possible," is among Arendt's better-known interpretations of conditions in a totalitarian state. This, a state of exception par excellence, is the defining objective of total domination, she tells us. Arendt is writing about the sovereign's claim to infinite prerogative, to put the point another way. Baraitser's claim to sovereign prerogative is quite the same. Everything was possible in Baraitser's courtroom—or, at the very least, no limit to the possible was tested. Are we not on notice that we all live within this condition? The sovereign can torture and it is not torture: Assange in captivity demonstrates this plainly enough. At the extreme—and the extreme has been reached numerous times in numerous cases—the sovereign can kill and it is not murder.

◆ ◆ ◆

Not long after Julian Assange's arrest, an organization called Speak Up for Assange began circulating a petition asking journalists to support "an end to the legal campaign against [Assange] for the crime of revealing war crimes." The document is offered in eight languages. At writing it bears 1,400 signatures, mine among them, from ninety-nine nations.

To gather fourteen hundred journalists in behalf of Assange is an excellent thing. But when we put this number against the number of journalists in the ninety-nine countries cited—there are more than thirty thousand in America alone—we must draw a different conclusion. Where is everybody? we must ask. What happened (and when), such that the press that welcomed Assange and WikiLeaks after its founding in 2006 came to evince nearly rabid animosity toward both?

If 2010 marked WikiLeaks's coming of age as a publisher, it was also the year the American press, along with media in Britain and elsewhere, began to turn on their former colleagues. The precipitating event was the October publication of "Iraq War Logs." It was on this occasion that official Washington established three long-running themes: WikiLeaks risks American lives; WikiLeaks compromises national security; WikiLeaks aids those the United States deems adversaries. The American press concurrently began to shift its attention from the publications it had enthusiastically reproduced to WikiLeaks and its founder. Reports of internal dissent, financial difficulties, and Assange's allegedly abrasive personality

52 · RARITAN ON WAR

date to this time. An unrelenting campaign of character assassination had begun.

In the ensuing years the press and broadcasters have treated us to a truly preposterous list of Assange's shortcomings, disorders, excesses, and perversities. He is a rapist, a narcissist, a megalomaniac, a fascist. He is a liar, he is unwashed, and he did not clean his bathroom at the Ecuadoran Embassy—where he mistreated his cat and smeared feces on the walls. Caitlin Johnstone, the irreverent Australian commentator, gathered twenty-nine such entries and offers replies to them as her contribution to *In Defense of Julian Assange*. To read her list is to confront the extent to which American media have made a pitiful mockery of themselves, a juvenile spectacle worthy of *Lord of the Flies*. Entirely out the window, of course, is any further consideration of the war crimes and corruptions reported in "Iraq War Logs" and other releases.

On 13 April 2017, shortly after President Trump named him director of the CIA, Mike Pompeo addressed the Center for Strategic and International Studies (CSIS), the Washington think tank. Pompeo devoted a remarkable proportion of his speech to WikiLeaks and Julian Assange. This reflects the timing of Pompeo's CSIS presentation. Less than a year earlier, WikiLeaks had begun publishing mail stolen from the Democratic National Committee's computer servers. By the time Pompeo spoke, the convoluted, devoid-of-evidence fable we call "Russiagate"—a cockeyed conspiracy theory if ever there was one—was fixed in the American consciousness. "It is time to call out WikiLeaks for what it really is—a nonstate hostile intelligence service often abetted by state actors like Russia," Pompeo asserted.

This was Pompeo's essential message that day. The press and the broadcasters turned it into headlines, and another groundless bit of fabrication was on its way to being accepted as fact. The conjured connection with Russia was key. It licensed many in the press, and I would say most mainstream media, to abandon Assange, so finishing what it had begun years earlier: much that we find on

Johnstone's list of slurs dates from the time since Assange was identified as neither a journalist nor a publisher but as a foreign agent with some indeterminate tie to Moscow.

In Defense of Julian Assange gives us an excellent, well-edited record of a pilgrim's progress as he fights our very necessary war against runaway secrecy in defense of properly democratic societies whose governments operate transparently. Daniel Ellsberg, Patrick Cockburn, John Pilger, and Matt Taibbi are among the book's many distinguished contributors. Renata Avila, a Guatemalan human-rights lawyer who has represented Assange over many years, writes a cogent account of meeting Assange (in Budapest, 2008), during which he explained WikiLeaks's working principles: decentralization, security (of staff and documents), and protection of sources. Stefania Maurizi, an Italian journalist and longtime WikiLeaks collaborator, describes, albeit discreetly, the organization's operations from the inside out. There are repeated challenges to the by-now-baroque edifice of falsehoods erected to turn Julian Assange into one of the repellent malefactors of our time.

If *In Defense of Julian Assange* offers a factually sound understanding of the WikiLeaks founder and the truth-seeking tradition he stands within, it is also useful as a mirror to reflect upon the commonly accepted story of the man and his work. To read the book is to recognize that our corporate media's over-the-top renderings of Assange are best understood as "persecution texts." This term belongs to René Girard, the late philosopher and social critic. Persecution texts are accounts of transgressions told from the perspective of those persecuting the transgressor. They typically combine the real and the imaginary, the true and the false, and they are reliably replete with "characteristic distortions." Of these distortions Girard tells us something very useful. Even if they are ridiculous (as in the Assange case), there is much to learn from them. The more ridiculous the text, Girard finds, the more it tells us about its authors. "The unreliable testimony of persecutors," Girard writes, "reveals more because of its unconscious nature."

54 · RARITAN ON WAR

Our question is clear: What do the very numerous persecution texts available to us reveal about the media that compose and publish them? It is not enough to see the pitiful and juvenile in press reports of scatological doings at the Ecuadoran Embassy, or of cruelty to a housecat, or of an unclean loo. These are texts. What do we find as we interpret them?

In the American context, our media have made Assange the object of a purification ritual. In this his persecution—and so I will call it—is in line with the Quaker hangings in Boston, 1659–1661, the Salem witch trials three decades later, the anti-Communist paranoia of the 1920s and 1950s, the Russophobia and Sinophobia that now beset us. In all such cases, the righteous community—transcendent, messianic, chosen—has been corrupted and must be regenerated, its purity restored. The polluting alien must be expelled. Hardly is it difficult to read this unconscious drive, primitive as it is, into our media's obsessions with Assange the unclean, with Assange who is a Russian asset, with Assange who is not a journalist.

Girard would consider Assange a scapegoat in his highly developed use of this term. Assange in sequestered captivity is a sacred outcast, to put the point another way. This ever-perplexing figure has a history extending back to the Romans and has since inspired many interpretations and reinterpretations. The sacred outcast (*homo sacer* in Latin) is "noble and cursed," in Girard's phrase. He is considered worthy of veneration, but he is also a breaker of taboos and so is subversive of the established order. The admired transgressor: this will do as a thumbnail description to get us past a contradiction that is merely apparent, the holy man who must be cast out. By tradition the *homo sacer*, important to add, can be murdered without fear of retribution. This, too, is a feature of his fate.

The sacred outcast serves an essential function. In the time before he is ostracized, the threat of division, schism, or even violence hangs over the group to which his persecutors belong. A certain hysteria commonly besets the group during this crisis phase. Ejecting the *homo sacer* relieves these pressures. Differences within the group are dissipated. I will return shortly to this point.

Assange as archetype: We can gain much understanding if we use this thinking—judiciously, of course—further to illuminate the media's treatment of him. If the righteous community has banished the transgressor from its midst, what was the transgression? *In Defense of Julian Assange* stands with the signature-seeking website on this point: Assange's crime is to expose the crimes of the powerful. This is fine but not enough. The press and broadcasters have impurities of their own to bleach clean. What are these?

Assange the scapegoat has departed from the originary American code. This is his irreducible violation. He broke the taboo against questioning—prominently, in public space—the essential virtue of American intent and American power. Many of WikiLeaks's major document releases—not all—challenge this sacrosanct precept. American media, with occasional and carefully attenuated exceptions, observe it, so staying well clear of the taboo. The originary code amounts to a code of silence at this point, so many are the instances of malign American conduct that go unreported (or dishonestly reported) by our corporate-owned newspapers and broadcasters. When Assange confronts the fallacy of American goodness and innocence, he also confronts the media's sycophantic allegiance to official orthodoxies. In effect, he exposes the media's culpability—its collaboration in preserving the myth necessary to obscure the true nature of American power.

How shall we understand those early years, when the press readily republished WikiLeaks's releases? After the publication of "Iraq War Logs," the *New York Times* set up an interactive site called "The War Logs." It featured a search mechanism enabling readers to sift through the immense inventory of documents according to topic. This was diligent journalism in the new mode. *Al Jazeera* was the only other media outlet to match the *Times* for thoroughness. It is true that the *Times* concurrently published news reports

56 • RARITAN ON WAR

that erased the complicity of U.S. forces in the torture of Iraqi detainees, leaving readers to conclude the Iraqi military and police acted without the knowledge of American authorities. But the question remains: How did the press go from collegial collaboration with Julian Assange to scapegoating him as a pariah? It is a very curious journey by any measure.

American media, shelters of our indoctrinated elites, were fated from the first to face a choice in their relations with WikiLeaks and its founder. Sooner or later, working with the organization was bound to put them at odds with the institutions of power they had long and loyally served. There was the potential for conflict, crisis, or both—schism or violence in the archetypal meaning of these terms. Sooner or later, they would have to decide whether to continue observing the originary code or to transcend it, as Assange had done to such impressive effect.

The moment to choose arrived with the release of "Iraq War Logs." So did the disavowals and demonizing begin—the casting out and scapegoating. And so was harmony restored between the press and the institutions of power it reports upon. It was inevitable that all the persecution texts would follow.

Now we come to the truth of our media's remarkable animosity toward Assange. Journalism is seeing and saying; WikiLeaks and its founder are exemplary practitioners by this irreducible definition of the craft. The work is to see and say in the cleanest possible fashion—with gathered facts alone, without editorial comment, without persuasion. In this way Assange stands as an ideal—never mind whether our corporate media so acknowledge him. In archetypal terms he is sacred. But Assange is also damned, for he is a traitor, just as he is accused. He is unfaithful to our mass media's illusions, and we must consider these two ways. There are the illusions our press perpetuates in its pages, and of these there are of course very many. There are also the illusions media live within—illusions of integrity, of impeccable ethics, of principled independence from institutions of power. Mainstream media have long deceived themselves with these illusions, and it is these Assange betrays. He betrays, then, those who warrant betrayal.

So is Assange banished. So should we understand his banishment. Assange has preserved the lost ideals his persecutors recognize, with unconscious but legible bitterness, as no longer their own. It is by casting him out that the righteous community averts dangerous conflicts in its ranks and restores the existing order, the troubled peace Assange has so honorably disturbed.

Summer 2020

Six Years from Afghanistan
MICHAEL MILLER

Only in his dream does he forget
That his rifle was used for killing.
Only in his dream does he dismantle his M16
With the same care that his hands
Once bestowed upon his dying mother
In her house in Wilmington, North Carolina,
Where he searched for pieces of
Broken glass smoothed by the sea,
His polished treasure on the rippled
Sand at low tide. If only he were that
Boy in his dream and not an ex-marine
Dismantling his rifle and loving the parts,
The trigger, the bolt, that he cleans
To perfection; he does not assemble them
Into the weapon he used to kill
The Taliban who kept on coming,
Who will always be coming.

Winter 2018

The Road to Revolution
C. FELIX AMERASINGHE

On 27 January 2009, Arunachalam Mahadevabalasingham, who would later appreciate being called Bob, pores over a chess set in his grandparents' shack, which doubles as a coconut stall. Aruna is seven; his brother, Balu, is thirteen. Their childhood home was a concrete four-bedroom in Jaffna town, but that territory is now controlled by the Sinhalese-dominated Sri Lankan Army. The stall is a temporary slot for a family that is being driven from the upper point of Sri Lanka's teardrop form to the eastern coast.

At age five, Aruna had watched his parents shot by balaclava-masked cadres of the Tamil Tigers, their supposed protectors. Slippers still marked by his parents' sweat lay scattered on the street as their bodies were strung from a lamppost, a reminder to other Tamils of the penalty for trying to smuggle boys away from possible child conscription. Aruna's heart had caved watching the town carry on unmoved. Fishmongers called out the daily catch and durian vendors whipped forward on bicycles, indifferent to the shadows under the lamppost. The war was twenty-five years old. The only bodies that mattered were of close friends and family; others were discarded mannequins.

Now Aruna's older brother rubs his hands together in joy as he promises to explain a new chess opening. The Spanish variant of the Four Knights. "You'll love this one." He places the knights in their aggressive postures and asks Aruna to guess what should happen next.

But Aruna's concentration splits as the army checkpoint far up the street explodes. Chess pieces vibrate, roll, and cling together by their magnetic bases. Two Tiger cadres burst in. Their fingers caress the triggers of AK-47s. Balu snaps the miniature chessboard shut, capturing as many pieces as he can, and the brothers grab

60 • RARITAN ON WAR

their prepacked suitcases. The Tigers are on the move again and cloak themselves with a human shield of Tamils. Balu and Aruna, civilians under Tiger control, advance as pawns.

◆

On 15 March, Balu observes his younger brother. Aruna's hands are blistered, but he can tolerate the pain of gripping his switch-blade tight. The boy has a toughness that makes Balu hopeful, even while he senses his own end approaches. The Sri Lankan Army has shinier guns and sharper aim these days. Tiger counterattacks falter, and the group searches for fresh meat to toss into the onslaught.

◆

The scrub jungle thickens, and the boys become invisible. They live in squalor and are wrapped in a heat that is as wet as a cloud. Nightly, they play chess with missing pieces replaced by marked stones.

They pick their way between bombed-out shacks and burning water towers. Mankulam, Puliyankulam, and Kilinochchi, wasted by Sri Lankan artillery fire: these are the Tamil-majority ghost towns. From puddled elephant tracks, mosquitoes rise carrying dengue. Ranks thin as people die and are buried, Aruna's grandparents among them.

◆

On 15 April, Balu disappears. Every last teenage boy vanishes with him. Aruna braces their chess set tight to his chest as he marches, pulling his bag, receiving help from elderly men when he tires. He recalls his brother's dark hands laying out the pieces. Aruna revisits their games as he walks, listing the coordinates of each move to give himself purpose.

◆

On 8 May the Tamil masses reach a one-mile strip of eastern beach where, during past ceasefires, young couples of all ethnicities once watched the gliding tail fins of blue whales. An army advances on one side; a frigid ocean promises drowning on the other. And, in the sky, Sri Lankan Air Force bombers outnumber the many clouds. Mortar shells rain down with monsoon intensity.

Under each shell, the ground pops like a pressed blister. Aruna runs, although running is meaningless because there is no safe quarter on the beach. He focuses, in the seconds of calm, on the details around him: the shifting shapes of the sand, the flames that lick the wheel wells of buses, and the twists in eyebrows distorted by fear. These details keep him distracted, keep him alive.

Eleven days it lasts. Before the Tiger brass surrenders and is summarily executed.

◆

Aruna latches on to a Jesuit leading a flock of orphans. Thirty minutes from the devastated beach, they arrive at a clay riverbank. On the slope sit dozens of naked teenage Tamil boys. They protrude like crooked roots from the slopes. Soldiers break bones with rods. The boys whimper but do not squeal. Their bare ribs wither and recede in contrast to the firm uniforms of the Sri Lankan soldiers. Hems of camouflage hug biceps, enlarging the muscles. Big men; disappearing boys.

A middle-aged Tiger colonel, recognizable from propaganda posters, stands at the edge of the bank. His hunched figure is naked, bound, and bruised. Female army officers brush shoulders with the colonel for photographs. They chatter in Sinhalese, a language incomprehensible to Aruna. He shivers as they pass around cell phones, posing as if with a husband and confirming after that the shot flatters. Aruna has passed many female Sri Lankan soldiers, expecting at least a moment of motherly attention, but none of them offer him a smile or a pat on the head. Invisibility keeps him safe, but their dismissal feels unnatural. Like an insult.

As the priest presses him forward, Aruna notices a boy who must be his brother. The likeness is striking. And the boys' eyes meet. But

62 • RARITAN ON WAR

Balu's gaze is stoic, lost, as if he is in a coma. Aruna feels pressure behind his eyes. He pulls his bag with one hand, clutches the chess set with the other. Wheels of dust obscure the road ahead. People limp forward: an anonymous crowd. With no partner to teach Aruna, the rattle of the chess pieces connotes a permanent loss.

◆

Balu cannot bring himself to acknowledge Aruna. He imagines himself kneeling to offer a few words of advice: find people to love you, play chess because it is an immortal game, and keep sliding between obstacles. But that conversation must remain a dream. He tries to dilute his gaze and wipe his mind clear of the details that give life texture. Soldiers refill their rounds, metal chambers click, and death is minutes away.

◆

Aruna escapes the island on an overcrowded boat. He cleans toilets in Rameshwaram, South India, and sells sparklers in the south of France; in Spain, he obtains a fake passport and patrons until he lands in Canada with a Sinhalese man, Nishan, who becomes his actual father, according to forged papers. A man betrothed to a Sinhalese grocer in the Chicago suburb of Rogers Park.

Nishan is an accountant from the multiethnic eastern Sri Lankan town of Batticaloa. Neither the Tigers nor the Sri Lankan Army ever hassled him. Although the war had raged on the city outskirts, he had never felt the gaze of a gun or marched through jungle foliage. His fortunes sank from poor calculations. He looks for a new beginning but wears like a soaked sweater the fact of his failure, the shame of not having an excuse.

◆

They land, nest, in a Chicago apartment with incomplete sets of furniture. Symbols of the Sinhalese fill the dusty corners: statues of large-eared Buddhas, packets of jaggery sugar labeled with curvaceous Sinhalese script that Aruna cannot read, and peacock-feather fans. But Nishan's wife, Kamini, is kind. She is building an empire of Sri Lankan grocery stores. The family is rising into the middle class. For the first time in his life, Aruna tastes chocolate.

Kamini chain-smokes in the family room. Ashtrays fill with the remnants of wrapped tobacco. She talks with Nishan about inventory and taking out the trash, scrawls to-do lists on Post-it Notes. But she often describes things she likes as sexy. The building on Devon Street where she wants to buy a three-thousand-square-foot store; the strip lighting that has a blue hue; the wicker lounger: all so sexy. She brings color into the dullness.

♦

Nishan struggles with even simple tasks like submitting advertisements for the local papers. His new wife looms over him, and he obsesses about the size of his penis, which shrinks in response to the stress and seldom rubs against his pants.

Nishan remembers Canada, waiting with Aruna for their new identities to form. He would return from a day of assisting a plumber under the sink and bring a bag of fries to the highway-skirting motel where they stayed. Aruna's smile illuminated the room, and his black fingers glistened with salt. A quiet boy who often seemed folded up into his thoughts. Those were tender moments. The wrappers would uncrumple and crackle inside the Burger King bag, a sign of more food and that things can continue even after they seem finished.

♦

In third grade, 2011, nine-year-old Aruna struggles with formal reading and writing. His parents hire a tutor, a white woman with jet-black hair that smells of mango conditioner. She visits their home and gives Aruna writing exercises. Aruna divides the woman up into segments. The hair belongs to his mother. The cheeks around her smile

64 · RARITAN ON WAR

are his brother's. When the bare flesh of her calves brushes his shins, it reminds him of how he used to nestle in group hugs in shared beds.

And so Aruna loves this tutor, but from a distance. He tells her that English is a sexy activity and she corrects him: young boys should never call anything sexy.

He writes about leading a fair-skinned Tamil girl to safety through a downpour of shrapnel. Aruna describes the length of the girl's legs and the roundness of her belly. A thrill zips through him as he writes: "Her hair curled around her neck like midnight sweeps around the globe." The tutor underlines the sugariest phrases but explains that women don't need to be rescued or reduced to body parts. His story would be so much better if the girl fought alongside him. Tossing nunchakus, perhaps, or delivering karate kicks. The tutor flings her arms into a yoga Y and, inhaling deeply, declares Aruna brilliant. For that reason, he can master these vital principles of storytelling at a young age.

Aruna imagines snapping off the tutor's coconut-milk-colored nose. War had taught him the value of body parts, the attraction of their health, and he had spent his life waiting to be rescued. How could someone he respects find flaws in these ideas? He yearns to touch his mother's and his brother's intact bodies and give them proper hugs before goodbye. Be at peace while others rally around him for once. Aruna polishes his reading and writing twice as fast as he otherwise would have, just to be done with his tutor.

♦

These are things that make Aruna panic: the shriek of airplanes; the shine of guns on television; and the touch of a woman, not only because it reminds him of his mother but also because he remembers the Sinhalese soldiers and their photographs. Sometimes, the sound of Balu's miniature chessboard unlatching makes him go cold because Balu will never sit across from him again.

These are things that comfort Aruna: the creamy scent of cashew curry; a known endpoint to events, which signifies certainty; and Nishan's hand on his shoulder. Sometimes, the click of that chess set unlatching soothes him because he recalls his brother's voice offering advice. He remembers his mother and father leaning over to study their games in Jaffna and imagines a sheet of sari or a sleeve rubbing against his neck.

◆

In fourth grade, 2012, ten-year-old Aruna meets Finch Small, whose red hair frames a face that always seems dirty. Finch's thick parts—calves, shoulders, and cheeks—are often bruised bluish gray. His father, Finch reports, drinks three tall pints of Guinness, sometimes nursing all three at the same time. The man's day job is watching online poker.

Finch and Aruna play flick 'em marbles at lunch. The game reminds him of how he and Balu used to bounce a tennis ball to each other in slow moments in their grandparents' shack. Small spaces demanded fast reactions.

◆

A teacher jokes that Aruna's name would read easier if he were called Bob. And Aruna adopts the name Bob because Arunachalam Mahadevabalasingham, which had remained his first and middle names, are Tamil words. Linguistic identifiers that made him a target during a lifetime of war in Sri Lanka. And Bob now loves neutrality.

◆

The county sends an art therapist to work with Bob. He sketches palmyra trees and sunsets behind the Jaffna lagoon. His memories flood these simple images, but the therapist reacts as if they are empty. She tells him to burrow deeper, so he sketches his brother

66 • RARITAN ON WAR

in the window, his father peeling a banana, and his mother reading
Winnie-the-Pooh to teach him English.

The art therapist says Bob is holding back. So, he draws three
Tamil girls strapped with suicide vests, hurtling toward a fleet
of school buses. The caption reads, "hero run blow bus," even
though he knows the grammar is incorrect. In fact, he does not
associate suicide bombing with heroism at all. It leaves black
holes in families: empty chairs at the dinner table and bedrooms
filled with toys and journals that sit still, unloved, and then fade
away. Satchels and fenders survive bombings when children do
not. But Bob gives the therapist what she wants, so "hero run
blow bus."

These are the events that unfold after the art therapist approves
of Bob's drawing: a psychiatrist replaces the psychologist who
has long treated Bob; the guidance counselor explains the warning
signs for future gun-violence perpetrators; Principal Georgia
Devlin sends a gift of Ceylon tea; the school security officer, Illford
Gip, promotes the Boy Scouts and the therapeutic experience of
tying a slipknot; and the sheriff's department searches the family
computer, unearthing only Nishan's "wedged-panty" pornography
collection, which the officers delete.

◆

Nishan witnesses how the procession of officials isolates the boy,
who spends ever more time at the computer. Nishan fantasizes
about stomping in his oversized galoshes before kicking them out
the door. But he freezes; his incompetence would trip him up. If
only his Batticaloa house had been confiscated by the army, his
dog shot by the Tigers, or his life threatened by the husband of
some gorgeous woman with whom he'd had an affair: any legitimate excuse for fleeing. But that is not how it was. He simply
couldn't keep the numbers straight. He feels he lacks the moral
right to seize control, so he retreats to his shower to masturbate, to

enlarge his two-inch penis to three inches while dreaming that it has a horse's length.

◆

At recess on 9 May 2012, Bob huddles next to Finch Small as the 777s fly over toward O'Hare International Airport. "My father says that the scientific word for Indian is Sand N***er." Finch crushes a Cheeto loudly between his teeth and smacks his hands together to indicate a friendly provocation.

"You know for sure that that's bullshit."

"Yeah, but I guess I'd love it if you'd just kill the asshole. You must have killed people during the war." Finch's wry smile emphasizes the darkness in him. That darkness had accompanied Bob in the watery jungle heat, whispered sweet nothings to him when he felt hopeless on that beach in the final days of the war, and promised to clear the brush so that he could find eternity. But Bob had turned death away: a firm breakup. And now, even as he dreams of slitting Finch's father's throat with the switchblade the army had confiscated, he tells Finch it wouldn't be worth the art therapists that both of them would have to deal with afterward, never mind the jail time.

◆

On 20 September 2013, Kamini washes plates that Nishan forgot to clean. She thinks of the suicide-bomber drawing and the white noise of the heating unit becomes the hum she'd heard in the aftermath of bombings. In the capital city of Colombo, her hometown, Tiger bombers had left the city moth-eaten with loss. Every block became defined by places where lives had been destroyed: the Central Bank, the Office of Taxation, the Borella Buddhist Temple. And the fissures spread to the Otter Club, where her favorite cousin would no longer order Sinha beer at the bar; to her deceased aunt's house, where no surviving family member knew the hiding place

68 · RARITAN ON WAR

for the ancestral wedding sari; to the Sinhala Union pool, where the water would never again split with quite the force of her friend Paul Delivera's cannonball dive. She'd left Sri Lanka in part to escape those widening gaps.

But Kamini realizes that Bob has lived through an all-encompassing kind of loss. And she wants to tell Bob that Sri Lankans on every side were so cornered that their only choices dripped with evil. But he should not talk to all these hippies. They will never understand. What's more, one of them might ferret around and realize that a Sinhalese boy should not be so familiar with suicide bombers or speak Tamil. Art and writing are exposure. His false identity is a thin wrapping, one that relies on how ignorant Americans are of the war.

She approaches Bob, who sits at the computer. Electronic chess pieces drift across the screen, chirping as they land. Blue light fills his focused eyes. He moves the pieces of his miniature chess set, including the marked stones, in sync with the screen. Practicing the matches of the masters.

"Bob." Kamini wipes a tear from the edge of her eyelid and discards her planned line of conversation. "If you could have anything you want, what would it be?"

He remains fixated on the screen but mumbles, "That they write 'Bob' on my gravestone."

Kamini winces: How can she respond to that? The next day she buys Bob a large chess set, one whose pieces are heavy enough to withstand the hustle-bustle of classroom activity. This gift accompanies a Star Wars lunch box. Children should be children, she thinks, especially the ones who have moth-holed childhoods.

◆

At lunch the next day, Bob and Finch play chess. Bob teaches his friend the Spanish Knights opening, but it is too advanced. He has first to instruct how to advance a pawn and make the knight leap.

Bob struggles to explain, and he wishes he had Balu's easy way of teaching. For the first time, he talks to Finch about Balu.

"Before the war got really crazy, my brother, Balu, had a side job fixing motorcycles, adjusting them to take kerosene when gasoline was banned. He was good with his hands." Bob is surprised at the clarity of his own English. The words wing out from him. "In fact, it's ridiculous how much still happened while the war was hot."

"Like what?" Finch leans in so that his nose is almost against Bob's cheek. Goose bumps ripple along Finch's neck.

"Well." Bob smiles at his recollection of Jaffna resisting, persisting, through its routine. "I mean, kids attended school. They took exams. All while you could be kidnapped and sent to the front line by Tiger guerrillas."

"You had gorillas in Sri Lanka?" Finch squints, itches his armpits, grunts, and spins in a circle.

"Um. No. Guerrilla as in terrorist. The kind that put a bullet in your head if you talk back. There's nothing funny about this."

"Sorry." Finch squirms in discomfort. "How did your brother die?"

"Tiger killed him first," says Bob, "and then the Sri Lankan Army killed him."

"He died twice? I just shat my pants," said Finch, smiling, as if numb to the whole concept of losing someone. As if unable to grasp it.

"Gross." Bob punches his friend midshoulder. But they are chuckling. Outside, a boy trips and then leaps around like a kangaroo under fire, clutching his leg. Falling had never before been funny to Bob. It warranted concern. Now he sees the humor in the clumsiness and foolishness of it. Bob's shoulders relax, and the world seems a little lighter, a little crazier.

◆

70 • RARITAN ON WAR

Principal Georgia Devlin, who had seen Martin Luther King speak at the Mall in Washington, plans fifth-grade graduation. Bob in particular deserves recognition, so she insists that, in the program, two asterisks appear next to the names of students who received at least three A+s. Bob's name alone will enjoy those marks of fame.

Principal Devlin decrees that children will not receive graduation certificates. Instead, they will walk up in descending order of height, pause for five seconds on stage, and then file onto the risers. Tallest children stand at the top; smallest at the bottom. Applause must wait for the end. Absolute silence until then. To preserve decorum.

◆

The back of the line is packed with Asians whom they call late bloomers but who may never blossom past five foot three. Treh Than holds down the rear behind Ming Lee, Ping Su, and Bob, who is therefore fourth from the end. Brian Cassoway leads the way. At five foot ten, wearing a suit and a square-tipped tie that rises into an hourglass knot, he towers over the school. He is not an enrolled student, but his twin sister, Nubie Cassoway, is. Immediately to Brian's right are two girls who seem to have vaulted over puberty and landed ripe for a spread in *Seventeen* magazine. Behind them, zit-faced preteens arrive on stage and hold their five-second smiles in morbid silence. Only the echo of rustling programs is audible; the parents respect the ban on applause.

◆

When Bob reaches the spotlight, he crosses his hands like a choir boy. In one fist, he clutches a rook and bishop from Balu's chess set. Nishan watches the boy's composure in amazement. He wants to clap until his hands wear each other down to the bones. But his days in Batticaloa sap at his will. He remains glued to his chair. Nishan senses his penis vanishing, the foreskin flapping around a void. It is a minor success for him just to raise his hand to rub his temple.

◆

Kamini fumes that Bob is so far back in the line. The boy has spent his life wandering in long lines. Now he has finally reached somewhere good, an endpoint, and they shove him to the back. Outrageous. Kamini has spent thirty minutes without smoking a cigarette and has to chew a toothpick to calm her nerves. She generally abides by rules, but now she claps her hands together and beats her right foot in a loud rhythm.

◆

Nishan, inspired into a sudden confidence, smacks his hands together in an off-rhythm flash. Wanting to outdo his wife, he stands on his chair and hoots until the chair snaps and he falls. He jumps on the next chair and continues with his hooting and one-legged leaping until that chair too fails. He loops along the empty back row, breaking chair after chair, and flutters sideways like a one-man domino exhibit.

◆

Bob remains still, exceeding his five seconds. Parents mumble that they too would have liked to applaud their babies, and it's a disgrace that, just because Bob is smaller and smarter and darker than the other children, his parents are allowed to cause all this commotion. It is not fair to Than and Su, who cannot enjoy their five seconds of silence. These parents, who rarely care about anyone other than their own children, become vocal advocates for the Asians in the back.

Principal Devlin's simple words crackle through the microphone: "Now, Bob, it is time to move along. Let's let young Jing take your spot." And no one but Ping notices the error in his name. Ping removes his right shoe and hurls it into the shadows of the

72 • RARITAN ON WAR

theater wings. The laughter from the short boys around him is contagious. So he chucks his left shoe into the crowd.

The teachers, who encircle the podium in card chairs, call out in unison for everyone to talk in their indoor voice.

◆

Nubie Cassoway stands two rows lower than her twin merely because she is nine inches shorter than him. That twist of fate is not her fault, no result of her agency, but a reality. She tears off her scrunchie, shakes out her hair, and lifts up the lower hem of her gown so that she can leap onto the riser and yell out, "Fuck you all, my brother doesn't even go to this school. And who gives a damn about this fifth-grade graduation anyway? Who put the tall kids up top?"

◆

Bob stands still. He maintains his smile, thinking of how good it feels when his parents stand and fall and cheer him in the auditorium.

◆

Brian Cassoway never wanted to attend the graduation. His mother had argued to the school board that Brian is at a disadvantage: his all-boys private school, Pooky Prep, runs straight through to twelfth grade and does not hold a fifth-grade graduation. Wouldn't it be nice for Brian to boast his striking Pooky suit while celebrating with the other children? The Cassoways sent potted floral arrangements to the board members, everything in de minimis quantities, just below the floor for bribery established by Illinois law.

Now Brian Cassoway, seeing how Bob's parents stand out despite their short stature, wants to be a leader too. Outdo the rest. So he removes his tie and rips open his shirt. The buttons pop off and spray into the lower rows. He grinds the festive air. The two girls beside him begin a vigorous rendition of the floss, swinging their arms so that they become vibrating maypoles caught in fast forward and reverse. A soft hand grazes Brian's thigh, and he longs to attend public school.

◆

Now comes Illford Gip, the retired police officer and onetime Army reservist who almost served in the first Iraq war. The school security guard. A skilled marksman, he spends hours dreaming of confronting a would-be mass shooter in a shopping mall. He would sneak in through a vent while wearing a black body stocking, and he would fire two shots, one to the head and one to the heart, killing the crazed shooter instantly. All the women in JCPenney—who resemble soft-lit supermodels—would strip off their clothes and absorb him into a massive orgy of gratitude.

Illford Gip, despite his dreams, when confronted with a real school shooter at a nearby middle school, will one day run in the opposite direction and, from the safety of a nearby portable potty, call in backup from the police station.

Illford Gip now charges Bob to force him onto the risers. But a sudden tremor runs through him. Bob does not flinch or glance at Illford Gip. The boy has a sturdiness and permanence, like those stone horsemen at roundabouts who reduce snowstorms to frosted icing while people cower in their homes. He changes course, preferring to chase other children into the stage wings. There, a boy pushes out the handle of a mop. Illford Gip trips, and as he falls toward his concussion, he ponders: Would I have been better served if I rappelled into the auditorium on a cable instead of charging the stage?

◆

Now sits Gilly Sandrison, who believes that graduations are feel-good nonsense. She wanted to take her precocious daughter to Mozambique to build houses for the poor instead, but the tickets were too expensive. So she knits a thick sweater and tastes her

74 • RARITAN ON WAR

bitterness while her daughter frolics in the stage wings. It is unfair that people assume she opposes the flu vaccine just because she wears white foundation and sings "You Are My Sunshine" while walking through the school. She gets her daughter vaccinated every year. She hears the din and observes the little brown boy. There might be something worth protesting here, even if she doesn't quite know what it is.

Gilly Sandrison stands, and her knitting needles prick her as they tumble down. She wants to be recognized as an experienced protester in her own right. But her knee-length hair catches in the joint of the chair and her neck takes a vicious whiplashing.

•

As children clear the risers and scatter through the audience, Bob waits for that familiar traumatic flinch from all the noise. But his nerves remain chilled. The scene has a lightness to it, like a torrent of children falling and getting up and jumping on one leg.

Although mass shootings will occur at several neighboring middle schools, none will occur at his. The two likeliest shooters, scarred by violent childhoods, had opted for a different opening move the first time Bob showed Finch how to advance a pawn. And with each passing lunch period, the steady march of fifth grade, the boys corrected their tilt toward violence.

Bob surveys his surroundings. Farther down his riser, Finch shields his eyes from the lights and smiles like someone who has just tasted melted caramel for the first time. His parents are absent from graduation, but the rising pulp of his cheeks indicates that it does not bother him anymore. Illford Gip remains flat on the ground, and several children play hopscotch over his thick figure. Gilly Sandrison is catching up, one hair at a time. Brian Cassoway gyrates while Nubie Cassoway punches the air. Kamini and Nishan chant, "We stand with Bob," and the auditorium thunders like a shifting elephant herd.

Bob hears the rhythm, the calmness, of his own breath. He imagines Balu standing across from him. "Very good," his brother says, waving a frail hand above a field of chess pieces. "Now draw in your last remaining castle, position your bishops, and attack with all the pawns that you've made into queens. Involve every piece. Finish this game. Then let's start another one."

Summer 2022

War and the Failures of the Fourth Estate
ANDREW J. BACEVICH

LET'S GET THE quibbles out of the way first. Mark Danner's *The Secret Way to War: The Downing Street Memo and the Iraq War's Buried History* hardly qualifies as a book—it is more of a pamphlet, a collection of documents supplemented with commentary. By my count, the author-written text is a mere seventy pages—small pages embellished with oversized margins.

Yet in compiling the materials that comprise *The Secret Way to War*, Danner has performed a notable act of public service. To read this book is to confront some of the most pressing questions of our day: What is the actual nature of the American political system? Even acknowledging the persistence of democratic rituals, to what degree can we meaningfully describe the United States today as a democracy? To what extent has our system of governance evolved into something quite different? And if it is different, what is that something? Since the "Global War on Terror" has been used as sufficient rationale to disregard or tacitly waive provisions of the Constitution, and since that war is expected to continue for decades or even generations (as President Bush has repeatedly warned), to what extent can we state with assurance that the United States remains or will remain a constitutional republic?

The Iraq War and, more broadly, the Bush administration's conduct of its war on terror have imparted considerable urgency to these questions. True, America's imperial pretensions had become manifest well before September 2001. Yet only since 9/11 have we begun to glimpse the moral, material, and political costs that erecting a global Pax Americana is likely to entail. Granted, the cult of the imperial presidency has roots extending back at least to the early days of the Cold War, if not to the Great Depression. Yet only now, as the Bush administration advances claims that "keeping America safe" requires a mandate of essentially limitless executive authority, are we beginning to understand the full consequences of allowing Congress to become, over the course of several decades, a marginal political force. As congressional fecklessness, corruption, and dysfunction have achieved stupefying proportions, the system of checks and balances has collapsed, perhaps irrevocably.

In *The Secret Way to War*, Mark Danner does not take up these matters directly, but they hover disconcertingly in the background. Danner's immediate concern is more specific. His focus is on President Bush's decision to invade Iraq, on the campaign of government disinformation orchestrated to justify that decision, and on the widespread journalistic malpractice that aids and abets such government efforts by keeping "political debate willfully stupid and opaque."

For Danner, clearing away the obfuscation surrounding Bush's decision for war—a preventive war at that—is not merely an academic exercise. He believes that persistent confusion about the war's origins—think about all those Americans still convinced that Saddam Hussein was complicit in 9/11—both exemplifies and serves to deepen the political crisis in which we are immersed. In this sense, Danner writes, *The Secret Way to War* is "a book not about what happened but about what is happening."

Danner is himself a distinguished journalist who teaches at Berkeley and Bard College and contributes regularly to the *New York Review of Books*. The lies and schemes of politicians dismay but do not surprise him. Far more troubling, in his view, is the fact that journalists should fail to expose those lies and schemes for what they are. To be sure, hardly a day goes by without the *New York Times* and the *Washington Post* revealing—even reveling in—corruption, stupidity, or misdeeds on the part of some hapless federal agency or official. But within days news becomes "old news" and some fresh scandal eclipses yesterday's outrage. Things are "brought to light," Danner writes, "and at the same time pushed back into the dark." The restless media spotlight moves on.

78 • RARITAN ON WAR

The net effect, Danner believes, is less to enlighten than to trivialize. Journalism today does not evoke a civic response; instead it conveys the impression that, whatever the latest malefaction, it really just amounts to politics as usual. The upshot, according to Danner, is that we find ourselves today living in "an Age of Frozen Scandal." Danner's gripe is not that present-day journalists keep the public in the dark about chicanery or dishonesty in the halls of government. Rather, it is that they convey the impression that there's nothing really to be done about it. As a consequence, citizens are overwhelmed by—and become numb to—a continuing "cycle of revelation, investigation, and expiation" that leads to nothing. Government malfeasance becomes like crabgrass. Lament it all you want, but halfway through summer it ruins your lawn. So live with it.

◆   ◆   ◆

Danner had explored some of these themes in his previous (and much larger) compilation of documents with commentary, *Torture and Truth: America, Abu Ghraib and the War on Terror* (2004). Accurately asserting that one of the effects of 9/11 had been "officially to transform the United States from a nation that did not torture to one that did," Danner ruminated over why evidence of that transformation had evoked only a passing and superficial reaction.

The stomach-churning documentation of U.S. troops gleefully taunting, tormenting, and brutalizing Iraqi detainees did momentarily qualify as a Big Story. Soon enough, however, that moment passed, and most Americans seemed to endorse President Bush's reassuring conclusion that the sordid events at Abu Ghraib "do not represent America." Within weeks, the press (along with the rest of the country) turned its attention elsewhere, working its way through a sequence of other transitory Big Stories: the Valerie Plame Affair, which involved the "outing" of a covert CIA agent in retaliation for her husband's opposition to the Bush administration; Hurricane Katrina; the indictment of Scooter

Libby for covering up his role in revealing Plame's identity; the revelation of a widespread government program of warrantless domestic surveillance; the Dubai ports deal; the row over illegal immigration; and so on.

Why this seemingly willful determination to minimize or even evade the implications of Abu Ghraib? Perhaps, Danner speculated, the horrifying images at the very center of the scandal provided a partial explanation. Instead of producing angry demands for accountability and corrective action, the pictures "had the opposite effect, helping to block a full public understanding of how the scandal arose." Finding the sheer ugliness just too much to bear, Americans found it necessary or at least more agreeable to look away.

Danner may have been right on that score, but there is another angle to consider, one related to the iconic status of the American soldier in present-day American life. After all, the perpetrators of torture and abuse at Abu Ghraib were not garden-variety hoodlums or gangbangers. They wore the uniform of the United States Army, which by definition meant that they embodied the very best that American society has to offer. So at least right-leaning politicians and pundits have asserted ever since the days of Ronald Reagan, and the Republican Party has reaped considerable benefit as a consequence. Eager to do likewise (and to make amends for having allegedly defamed soldiers during the Vietnam War), liberal politicians and pundits have happily chimed in.

But this enthusiasm for the American fighting man and woman does not derive from calculations of partisan advantage alone. For a nation deeply conflicted about its cultural trajectory, soldiers offer reassurance that the acids of modernity have not yet effaced all the emblems of remembered virtue. Even if the rest of American society obsesses about sex and celebrity and wallows in crass materialism, in the ranks of the U.S. Armed Forces, self-discipline, self-sacrifice, and patriotism survive. By the end of the twentieth century, Americans felt a compelling need to believe in this supposed reservoir of

80 • RARITAN ON WAR

national virtues, a need contributing to a tendency to inflate the significance of the victories that the U.S. military was racking up after the Cold War. Beating up on Manuel Noriega, Slobodan Milošević, or Saddam Hussein—or even gloriously losing a confrontation with Mohamed Farah Aideed—seemingly refuted the suspicion that America had become hopelessly lost in a swamp of decadence. Operations Just Cause, Desert Storm, Allied Force, Enduring Freedom, and Iraqi Freedom proved that the spirit of Bunker Hill and Valley Forge lived on.

As the Abu Ghraib scandal broke in public, it represented an affront to that comforting belief. True-blue soldiers were supposed to be like Private First Class Jessica Lynch, the girl warrior doing her utmost to promote the spread of freedom and democracy after 9/11. Now here was Private Lyndie England—the smirking pixie with a dazed, naked Iraqi on the other end of her leash. Who more accurately captured the spirit of George Bush's America: Jessica, the all-American blonde, or Lyndie, the demented sadist?

This was not a question that the president wished to entertain—hence, the alacrity with which he rendered his definitive judgment, announcing that Abu Ghraib represented the "disgraceful conduct of a few American troops" and nothing more. Although critics of U.S. policy, the Iraq War swelling their numbers, suggested that Abu Ghraib had exposed the dark underbelly of the American way of life or at least grew directly out of administration policies intended to "get tough" on terrorists, Bush was not having any of it and neither were most of his fellow citizens. Abu Ghraib was simply the work of a handful of bad apples: end of story.

For this reason, even as the events at Abu Ghraib became the subject of innumerable inquiries and commissions, the resulting reports reprinted verbatim in *Torture and Truth* amounted to very little. None of them—the Taguba Report, the Jones-Fay Report, the Schlesinger Report—made any real impact. The swarm of investigations worked better than a cover-up. They admitted the facts and then dispersed the responsibility. They acknowledged the damage to U.S. policy, but shielded the policymakers from accountability.

The capstone effort was the grandly titled Independent Panel to Review Department of Defense Detention Operations. Serving secretary of defense Donald Rumsfeld appointed former secretary of defense James Schlesinger to chair this group, which also included another former secretary of defense, a retired four-star general, and a hawkish former member of Congress. While it found errors of commission and omission aplenty, the Independent Panel wanted the buck stopped several thousand miles from the Pentagon. Culpability, it concluded, lay solely with the actual perpetrators of abuse. Schlesinger's pithy verdict: "It was kind of 'Animal House' on the night shift." Asked if Rumsfeld ought to resign in light of Abu Ghraib, Schlesinger rallied to defend the man who had allowed him one last moment in the limelight. For Rumsfeld to step down, Schlesinger declared, "would be a boon to all of America's enemies." Overall, it was a triumph of bureaucracy.

This bureaucratic triumph gutted the principle of accountability. An abundance of evidence showed that inadequate training, poor supervision, commanders playing fast and loose with service regulations and the Geneva Convention, and pressure from on high to get results no matter what had helped create the environment for Abu Ghraib. Yet these factors were noted only to be effectively dismissed. So Rumsfeld kept his job while Private England and her expendable comrades took the fall.

According to Danner, the real scandal of Abu Ghraib "is not about revelation or disclosure but about the failure, once wrongdoing is disclosed, of politicians, officials, the press, and, ultimately, citizens to act." Knowing is not the problem; it is responding to the facts staring us in the face. "The scandal is not about uncovering what is hidden," he concludes, "it is about seeing what is already there—and acting on it. It is not about information; it is

82 • RARITAN ON WAR

about politics." This is true enough, but the issue goes beyond mere politics.

◆   ◆   ◆

Danner himself knows that. In *The Secret Way to War* he focuses on the complicity of journalists in perpetuating the "Age of Frozen Scandal." His chosen instrument in this effort is the so-called Downing Street memo. This highly classified document summarizes a meeting of the British war cabinet, which Prime Minister Tony Blair convened on 23 July 2002 to discuss a prospective military confrontation with Iraq. Among other things, the meeting provided the occasion for Blair's key national security advisers—the foreign secretary, the minister of defense, the chief of defense staff, and the head of MI6 (the British foreign intelligence service)—to report on conversations with their U.S. counterparts. In short, the memo offers insight into what was really afoot in Washington.

The meeting occurred at a time when the Bush administration was publicly insisting that no decision for war had been made. Indeed, at this time and for months thereafter, the president was still devoutly expressing his hope that the United States could resolve its dispute with Saddam Hussein peacefully. In concise, direct, unambiguous prose—the British may have lost an empire, but they still know how to draft a minute—the Downing Street memo reveals Bush's expressions of restraint to have been a sham.

Although the document deserves to be read in full, four of its points are especially explosive. First, at a time when President Bush and his lieutenants were insisting in public that they hoped to avoid war, Foreign Minister Jack Straw was informing his colleagues that "Bush had made his mind up to take military action." Second, acknowledging that "the case [for war] was thin" and with an eye toward "help[ing] with the legal justification for the use of force," Straw proposed that "we work up a plan for an ultimatum to Saddam to allow back in the UN weapons inspectors," implicitly acknowledging that subsequent Anglo-American diplomacy in the

United Nations was designed not to prevent a war but to provide a suitable pretext for starting one. Third, in response to Straw's claim that "Saddam was not threatening his neighbors, and [that] his WMD capability was less than that of Libya, North Korea or Iran," Sir Richard Dearlove, the head of MI6, reported that Iraq's military intentions and capabilities were beside the point: within the Bush administration, "the intelligence and facts were being fixed around the policy"—a formulation guaranteed to gain Dearlove entry into future editions of *Bartlett's Familiar Quotations*. Fourth, with months of ostensibly serious diplomatic activity yet to come, Defense Secretary Geoffrey Hoon revealed that "the U.S. had already begun 'spikes of activity' to put pressure on the regime," a reference to the ratcheting up of air attacks against targets in Iraq, launched under the guise of enforcing the so-called No-Fly Zones. Hoon was really saying that in the summer of 2002, the war against Saddam, which had never really ended after Operation Desert Storm, was without fanfare resuming in earnest.

When the Downing Street memo was leaked to the *Sunday Times* of London in the spring of 2005, two years after the crisis had culminated in a full-scale invasion, it caused a considerable stir in the United Kingdom, then in the midst of an election campaign. In the United States, however, the memo garnered much less attention. For Danner, the lack of interest paid to it here qualifies as egregious journalistic oversight. Here, in his view, was the smoking gun. Here was proof positive that the Bush administration had, if not lied outright, at least "blatantly exaggerated the intelligence it was given to convince the country to go to war." Here lay evidence of duplicity and chicanery at the highest levels of government—malfeasance that produced a disastrously unsuccessful policy.

How could it be that in the dominant American media outlets—the prestige papers, the television networks, the weekly newsmagazines—the memo created barely a ripple? Danner faults the conventions of "balanced" journalism, which requires reporting both sides of the story with a straight face, even when one side

84 • RARITAN ON WAR

is obviously deluded or simply dissembling. Yet Danner also suggests that this pose of objectivity serves as a convenient cover for something much more insidious. The real problem with present-day journalists, at least in Washington—and the reason for their reluctance to confront the implications of a document like the Downing Street memo—is that they have been compromised. No longer seeing themselves as watchdogs serving the public, journalists have become part of the governing elite, insiders who are contemptuous of the plain folk ignorant of the way the game of politics really works. Inflated with self-regard, gratified to number themselves among those who are "in the know," they have a stake in perpetuating that game. Ensuring that the game's legitimacy should remain above question has emerged as a priority.

So while they needle, bait, and seek to embarrass the officials they cover—to elicit visible irritation or discomfort is to affirm their own importance—journalists go about their business in a way that preserves the illusion that our government is of, by, and for the people. Cynicism has supplanted skepticism as the reporter's distinguishing trait. Just as the politicians pretend to be public servants, devoted to the common good, so too the journalists pretend to dig relentlessly for the truth and the whole truth. As a result of the way it is practiced in modern-day Washington, writes Danner, journalism becomes "a deliberate impoverishment, a turning of inquiry and, at bottom, of curiosity into a dull and sterile game of black and white, played by rules that fail to reflect what anyone actually believes."

Danner's critique is not an entirely novel one. In her fine book *Canaries in the Mineshaft: Essays on Politics and Media*, Renata Adler offers a similar indictment of journalistic collusion with power, arguing the point at greater length and with far greater ferocity. Adler asserts that the "press itself has become a bureaucracy, quasi-governmental, and far from calling attention to the collapse of public process," it has emerged as "an instrumentality of the police function of the state." Danner's effective use of the Downing Street memo in *The Secret Way to War* confirms Adler's point. The inability or refusal of the U.S. media to recognize its significance testifies to their complicity in the state's policing function.

In the run-up to the Iraq War, the Bush administration had used the media for its own purposes. Members of the press had abetted a campaign of government deception and misinformation, with the notorious Judith Miller, star reporter of the *New York Times*, the most egregious offender.

Yet by the time the Downing Street memo revealed the scope of that deception, journalists, adhering to the reigning precepts of newsworthiness, had long since moved on to other things. They had little inclination to go back. Why revisit the machinations that had produced war when the war itself still raged? Weren't the bloody events actually unfolding in Baghdad and Fallujah of greater moment than discussions held two years earlier in the British prime minister's residence? To entertain the opposite view—to take the Downing Street memo at face value—was to invite troubling questions about the actual nature of a constitutional order that advertised itself as democratic and based on the rule of law. To admit the possibility that President Bush and his lieutenants had secretly decided in 2002 to launch a war of aggression and then, while publicly denying that any such decision had been made, had concocted a pretext for that war by manipulating and fabricating "intelligence" was to expose democratic politics as bogus. As for the vaunted Fourth Estate, it had not only failed to expose that fraud but had actually been complicit in perpetrating it. Rather than facing up to the implications of that failure, journalists—like the Americans who, confronted by the images of Abu Ghraib, preferred to look away— found it more convenient to classify the Downing Street revelations as unimportant, small stuff, "old news"—at most a one-day story.

As a consequence of this sort of journalistic irresponsibility, Danner concludes, we are "deliberately blindfolding ourselves." What we are blinding ourselves to, it seems to me, is that in matters related to national security, democratic practice has become little more than theater: for example, the October 2002 congressional resolution authorizing Bush to go to war (although the word "war" does not appear in the actual text of the resolution). The real politics occur behind closed doors, and citizens are allowed access only to whatever information the government chooses to make available. Real power is exercised by unelected officials who are more likely to feel a sense of responsibility to some interest group, faction, or bureaucratic institution than to the people. Within the inner circle of power, situations are created and then exploited. Decisions are made in secret and then merely announced, marketed as necessary to keep America safe, to win the war on terror, or to fulfill the American mission to advance the cause of freedom and human rights. When those decisions exact exorbitant costs or result in failure, protective mechanisms kick in to insulate the powerful from the consequences of their decisions. For its part, the press, all the while maintaining a pretense of watchfulness, plays along.

Half a decade into a global war expected to last indefinitely, what can we say about the health of the Great Republic? We can take comfort from the fact that, in a nominal sense at least, constitutional norms are still honored, democratic traditions are still observed, and appropriate homage gets paid to the rule of law. Yet it is increasingly difficult to say exactly where sovereign power has actually come to reside: surely it does not reside with the people. It becomes more difficult still to determine who benefits from the exercise of that power: surely it does not serve the common good.

Fall 2006

A *Translation from the* Aeneid
DAVID FERRY

Labores

Aurora rose, spreading her pitying light,
And with it bringing back to sight the labors
Of sad mortality, what men have done,
And what has been done to them, and what they must do
To mourn.

          King Tarchon and Father Aeneas together
Upon the curving shore caused there to be
Wooden funeral pyres constructed, to which
The bodies of their dead were brought and placed there,
In accordance with the customs of their countries.
The black pitch smoke of the burning of the bodies
Rose up high, and darkened the sky above.
Three times in shining armor the grieving warriors
Circled the burning pyres, three times on horseback
Ululating, weeping, as they rode.
You could see how tear drops glistened on their armor.
The clamor of their sorrowing voices and
The dolorous clang of trumpets rose together
As they threw into the melancholy fires
Spoils that had been stripped from the Latins, helmets,
And decorated swords, bridles of horses,
And glowing chariot wheels, and with them, also,
Shields and weapons of their own familiar
Comrades, which had failed to keep them alive.
Bodies of beasts were thrown into the fire,
Cattle, and bristle-backed swine, brought from surrounding

88 • RARITAN ON WAR

Fields to be sacrificed to the god of death.
And all along the shore the soldiers watched
The burning of the bodies of their friends,
And could not be turned away until the dewy
Night changed all the sky and the stars came out.

Over there, where the Latins were, things were
As miserable as this. Innumerable
Scattered funeral pyres; many bodies
Hastily buried in hastily dug-up earth,
And many others, picked up from where they fell
When they were slain, and carried back to the fields
Which they had ploughed and tilled before the fighting,
Or back into the city where they came from;
Others were indiscriminately burned,
Unnamed, and so without ceremony or honor.
The light of the burning fires was everywhere.
On the third day when the light of day came back
To show the hapless scene, they leveled out
What was left of the pyres and separated what
Was left of the bones, now cold and among cold ashes,
And covered over the ashes and the bones.

—book 11, lines 182–212

Summer 2014

◆ ◆ ◆

Percussion of Cut and Salve (2007)
M. FORTUNA

Oil, barbed wire, glass, netting,
grave dirt, and mica dust on canvas
(26 × 18 inches).

Summer 2014

White Fright (2017)
PETER LaBIER

Oil on canvas
(48 × 36 inches).

Summer 2018

Carbon Burn (2015)
RAY KLIMEK

Digital chromogenic print
(40 × 30 inches).

Fall 2017

god is water (1998)

d. mark levitt

Oil, acrylic, and oil stick on wood
(36×40 inches).

Summer 2003

Drawing for Transient Rainbow (August 2003)
CAI GUO-QIANG

Gunpowder on two sheets of paper
(179 × 159.5 inches).

Fall 2020

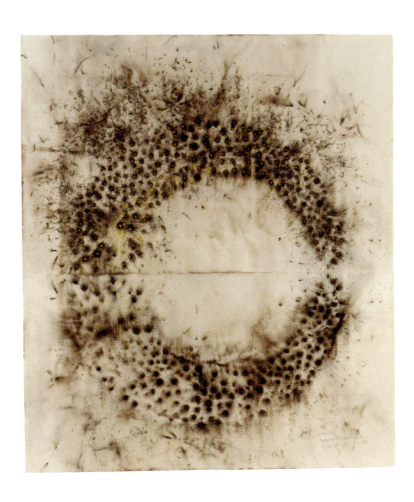

◆ ◆ ◆

Remembering Stalingrad
JOCHEN HELLBECK
Photos by EMMA DODGE HANSON

In 1927, when Franz Lehar composed his operetta *The Tsarevich*, he could not know that fifteen years later one of its songs would grow into a staple among the thousands of German soldiers pushing toward Stalingrad deep in Russia's south. "A soldier stands on the bank of the Volga, keeping guard for his fatherland . . ."—these words, the Germans felt, evoked their victorious stance, spurring them on to capture the city on the legendary river. Through the summer months of 1942, scores of armored German divisions rapidly advanced through the Ukrainian steppes and further east toward Stalingrad, sending the Soviet Army into headlong retreat. One year after the beginning of the German invasion, the Soviet regime appeared to be on the brink of collapse. On Stalin's orders, the city that bore his name was designated a fortress, and he commanded that it be defended to the last man. The industrial city of Stalingrad extends along the western banks of the Volga. "No land for us behind the Volga!" became the battle cry of the approximately fifty thousand Red Army soldiers of the Sixty-Second Army, who desperately sought to withstand the German onslaught.

As the battle for the city raged and Hitler grew impatient to capture it, the Soviet Army command planned a massive operation to encircle the Germans at Stalingrad. On 19 November 1942, one million heavily armed Red Army soldiers closed in on the three hundred thousand men of the German Sixth Army. Fixated on the possession of the city, Hitler ordered his army to hold out and await his rescue. After seventy more days of incessant fighting, the nearly one hundred thousand famished German soldiers that were still alive fell into Russian captivity. Of them, only six thousand returned to Germany after the war.

102 · RARITAN ON WAR

We located two dozen survivors of Stalingrad and visited them in their homes in Germany and Russia, to trace the memories of this pivotal battle of World War II in their faces and voices. Two of them are featured here, Anatoly Merezhko and Gerhard Hindenlang. In Stalingrad they came virtually face-to-face. As lieutenant in the Seventy-First Infantry Division, Hindenlang spearheaded the attack through the center of Stalingrad to the banks of the Volga in September 1942. Lieutenant Merezhko, after seeing his battalion bleed to death under the German assault, joined the staff of the Sixty-Second Army commanded by General Vassily Chuikov. The staff bunker was dug deep into the Volga's steep embankment, just north of Hindenlang's division.

Rendered on the pages to follow, the faces and words of these two veterans strikingly reveal the emotions and values that the war etched into them. Both offer precise recollections of personal turning points in this battle which would become a turning point in World War II. Each of them reflects with chilling precision the sense of detachment and isolation they felt amid ferocious fighting. Both also talk with great affection about their military commanders in Stalingrad whom they served as junior officers, an attachment that the images eloquently bespeak. Both comment on the enemy side with feelings of ambivalence, if not enduring resentment. And both dwell on the memory of the countless many who died around them in Stalingrad.

The images and thoughts we gathered powerfully evoke the enduring hold of the war over the lives of these veterans. Yet they also show marked differences in the ways Germans and Russians relate to the war today. Futility is the underlying tone of Hindenlang's testimony, as well as that of other German survivors, whereas fulfillment speaks through the words and portraits of Merezhko, and those of many other Red Army veterans. Before meeting with us, several of the Russians would ask us the same question: With uniform or without? They readily volunteered to slip into their parade gear and show their medals. The Germans were more reticent. Hindenlang was the only one to show us the signs of distinction he earned during the war, and he did so late into our conversation. Studied together, our encounters with Russian and German veterans give glimpses into the workings of two contrasting national cultures of memory: a broad sense of national sacrifice and pride in Russia, and haunting shadows of loss and defeat in Germany.

◆ ◆ ◆

ANATOLY GRIGOREVICH MEREZHKO

The high point of wild hatred toward the invaders, that was during our retreat across the Don River, and particularly on August 23 [1942]. On that day our officer school was practically wiped out. . . . At daybreak the [German] Fourteenth Panzer Corps broke through toward the northern districts of Stalingrad. And our neighboring battalion, it was entirely made up of cadets, got into their way. The German panzers drove up to their fortified defenses, and turning on their tracks they buried the cadets in the trenches. There was nothing we could do. We just watched. Around 1400 hours an armada of planes flies overhead, and the bombing of Stalingrad begins. We were forty kilometers outside of the city, and when it became dark we saw a steady glow in the sky. A fire so strong that the tip of the flames could be seen from forty kilometers away. And the planes went like this—the bombers coming in on lower altitude, and returning higher up. They would each make three, four raids, bombing the city to the ground.

On February 2 [1943], when we saw the long rows of German prisoners being led across the Volga into this endless Kazakh steppe, where the next settlement is at least fifteen or twenty kilometers away, we knew that there was no place for them to warm themselves. The frost was mild, it was only seven or eight [degrees Celsius] below zero, but when the wind blows from the Kazakh steppe, it pierces marrow and bone, it's piercing, repulsive wind.

Merezhko holding a book with a photograph of Marshal Vassily Chuikov, who commanded the Sixty-Second Army in Stalingrad.

Thousands of prisoners, marching in these long columns.... And you think: well, that's the end for you folks. But we also celebrated our victory. I remember, I was standing on the slope of the Volga, and at that very moment I vowed that I would remain alive until the end of the war. That's what I ordered myself: to stay alive until the end of the war!

Merezhko spoke with great veneration of General Vassily Chuikov, who commanded the Sixty-Second Army in Stalingrad. In an interview with the writer Vassily Grossman, who visited Chuikov at his command post in Stalingrad (Merezhko remembers accompanying Grossman to his meeting with Chuikov), Chuikov talked about the utter contingency of life in the "hell" of Stalingrad: "Here we count our lives in hours, minutes—that's honestly how it is." In mid-October 1942, when the battle for the city reached its highest

pitch, Stalin ordered front commander General Andrei Eremenko to leave his secure headquarters on the far bank of the Volga and to check on Chuikov and his men. In his great war novel Life and Fate, *Grossman records how Eremenko prepared for the mission. Before climbing on the boat that would take him across the Volga, the general walked up to a group of soldiers from a labor battalion and handed one of them his golden watch. The soldier didn't understand the meaning of the gesture and was stunned. In his conversation with us, Anatoly Merezhko talked about how the Battle of Stalingrad spurred similar gestures of trading material goods:*

In Stalingrad a tradition emerged that would take hold of the entire army. We called it "swapping without looking." A soldier runs into a fellow soldier or an officer. One of them places his hand on his pocket and says, "Let's swap without looking!" For instance,

108 • RARITAN ON WAR

you have some money in your pocket and he has a cigarette in his. You exchange them. Or an old watch that barely runs, and his watch is golden. That tradition came up because life in Stalingrad was measured in minutes, sometimes even in seconds. . . . The values from everyday life lost their meaning, they weren't worth a thing anymore. Within a matter of seconds you could be gone with your golden watch or your pockets stuffed with money. Sometimes a ruble note would be considered cheaper than the page of a newspaper. The newspaper you could use to roll a cigar, but the money was useless. That's how this habit formed.

After talking with us for hours, Merezhko invited us to the dining room where his wife had bedecked the table with hors d'oeuvres (zakuski) and drinks. Toasts were spoken over vodka, and Merezhko chose Stalingrad as the subject of his toast:

Stalingrad for me—that is my birth as a commander. Persistence, prudence, prescience, all the qualities required of a real commander. Love for your soldier, and memory of friends who died in battle and whom we could sometimes not even bury. We abandoned our dead as we retreated; often we couldn't even pull them into the trenches and cover them with earth. And when we were able to cover them with earth, the best monument was a shovel that we planted into a little earth mound and covered with the dead soldier's helmet. That is why Stalingrad for me is a holy ground. And when I meet with fellow Stalingraders or with people who show interest, who are truly interested in the history of the Battle of Stalingrad, I always relate to them with great respect. I try to be of help and, to the extent that I am able to, I try to remind our people and the entire world about the Battle of Stalingrad. To you, my friends.

◆

Anatoly Merezhko (b. 1921), a retired Colonel
General, died in December 2018 in Moscow.

Gerhard Hindenlang

While Merezhko and other Russian survivors take pride in the purpose of their lives as defenders of Stalingrad, German veterans struggle to identify a purpose in the battle, or the war as a whole. Gerhard Hindenlang vividly recalls the day of 14 September 1942, when his division pushed through the city center to the Volga and when his mission appeared to be accomplished:

Up there at the command post there were [Sixth Army commander Friedrich] Paulus and several other generals. They were waiting for me to come up and bring water from the Volga. When I came up they were completely disappointed that I came without a bottle in my hand. I reported that we could not go down there during daylight. As soon as we raise our nose over the bluff, the lead zings around our ears. How disappointed they were.

Four months later, on 26 January 1943, army commander Paulus and his staff sought refuge in the headquarters of the division where Hindenlang served as aide-de-camp to divisional commander Friedrich Roske. On 30 January, a radio message came in from the "Wolf's Lair," Hitler's East Prussian command point, promoting Paulus to the rank of General. The message was implicit but clear: never before in history had a German field marshal surrendered to the enemy. Roske sent Hindenlang to deliver the news to Paulus:

I went in, saluted, and reported that a radio message had come in and that he had been promoted . . . whereupon he says, "And now I am the youngest general in the army and must go into captivity." I was startled, because I thought, and Hitler of course, too, that he would commit suicide. He noticed that I was startled and asked me, "What do you think about suicide?" I said, "I don't think anything of it. I will command my troops until the last moment, and should I still be alive I will go into captivity with my troops.

Hindenlang showing the decorations he earned during World War II.

Hindenlang holding a photograph
of Fritz Roske, commander of the Seventy-First
Infantry Division.

To relinquish them to their fate—I won't do that." And then he said, "I am a Christian believer, I oppose suicide." But two weeks earlier he had said that an officer must not go into captivity. Back then that implied that he would commit suicide. So this is how he twisted this thing.

One day later, on 31 January, the Germans in Stalingrad surrendered to the Soviets. Declaring himself a "private individual," General Paulus recused himself from the talks, so as not to contravene Hitler's order to fight to the last bullet. Hindenlang's commander, Roske, conducted the negotiations on behalf of the army as a whole. This day began a long period of captivity, which ended for Hindenlang only in 1952. Roske, to whom Hindenlang remained personally attached, was among the very last Stalingraders to be

released in 1955. One year later, on Christmas Day 1956, Roske committed suicide. Throughout his years in captivity, General Paulus received special treatment from the Soviets who sought to make him into a spokesman of "antifascism." When he was brought back to East Germany in 1953, he was broken and ill, and he died in 1957.

On Germany's Day of National Mourning, a Sunday in mid-November 2009, we traveled to the town of Limburg, forty miles north of Frankfurt, where a thinning group of German Stalingraders comes together each year to commemorate the battle and mourn their dead comrades. It was on the cemetery of Limburg that we took this photograph (opposite) of Gerhard Hindenlang. He is shown standing near a granite shrine that bears the inscription "Stalingrad 1943."

114 • RARITAN ON WAR

*This was Hindenlang's last visit to Limburg. Only recently did
I learn about the history of the granite monument. I read about it
in the program calendar of one of the earliest meetings of the German Stalingrad veterans, in 1966. During the meeting one of the
veterans spoke about the symbolism of the shrine. Its shape and
granite core were to evoke the toughness of the Sixth Army and its
soldiers. The large bronze plate on top of the stone was chosen to
indicate the large number of "victims." Hidden below the plate was
a crystal shrine containing blood-drenched soil from Stalingrad.*

*The veteran went on, describing his and his fellow survivors'
feelings as they congregated around the monument. "The sacred
sacrificial flame lights up in the bronze plate, and we commune in
spirit with our comrades, the dead and missing Stalingrad soldiers
of the Sixth Army.... For a while we forget everything that sur-
rounds us, we are with them, fight and suffer, experience hunger
and cold, until the reality of everyday life tears us back. And we
want to repeat this pilgrimage to our Stalingrad monument until
the last one of us has fought his life struggle to the end, until the
last one of us has returned into his eternal homeland, until he has
come back to his comrades of the Sixth Army."*

•

Gerhard Hindenlang (b. 1916) died in March 2010
while preparing to dictate his memoirs.

Spring 2012

Make Movies, Not War
ELIZABETH D. SAMET

IN THE SUMMER of 1698, Louis XIV decided to stage a battle. The episode is recorded in the memoirs of that savviest of spectators, the Duc de Saint-Simon, who claims that the king had two principal motives, rendered here in Lucy Norton's translation: to "amaze Europe with a demonstration of his might," and to provide Madame de Maintenon "the pleasure of a splendid display of arms." Concealing these purposes under "the pretext" of teaching the young Duc de Bourgogne the "first principles" of war, Louis put him in nominal charge of a camp of sixty thousand soldiers at Compiègne and moved the entire court north from Versailles to watch the proceedings.

The participants competed with one another in the magnificence of their equipment and the abundance of their hospitality. Junior officers "ruined themselves" in the purchase of extravagant uniforms, while their superiors rivaled one another in the sumptuousness of their banquets. The field commander at Compiègne, the Maréchal de Boufflers, from whom the young duke was to learn the arts of war, was so sensible of the grand stage on which he acted that, according to Saint-Simon, he "astounded everyone by his liberality," schooling the king himself on "how to give royal entertainment." The feasting and pageantry carried on for weeks until the king, thinking it time to give Madame "a demonstration of everything that happens in war," at last issued the order to stage the siege of Compiègne. Assembled on a high rampart to watch the mock-assault on the fortress, members of the court could view "the whole plain and the dispositions of all the troops." It was, records Saint-Simon, "the most glorious sight."

While tens of thousands of French troops battled it out on the plain below, however, the spectators atop the rampart were

116 • RARITAN ON WAR

watching a different show altogether—"another sight . . . struck me so forcibly," writes Saint-Simon, "that forty years hence I shall be able to describe it as though it were yesterday." Madame de Maintenon had arrived on the scene in a sedan chair, the window of which she deigned only occasionally to open "four or five inches, never so far as halfway," so that the king, placing his hat on the top of the chair, was forced in rather undignified fashion to lean down in order to explain to her the maneuvers below. Saint-Simon was not the only courtier "far more taken up by this scene than by the movements of the troops." The faces of the onlookers "all had the same expression of ill-concealed apprehension and shamed astonishment" at the king's extraordinary solicitousness; "even the soldiers asked about the sedan chair," Saint-Simon notes, "so that it became necessary to silence the officers and discreetly prevent the troops from asking questions."

The carefully choreographed siege of Compiègne provided a marvelous set piece for Saint-Simon, who used it to illuminate the dynamic of watching and being watched that dominated the court of Versailles, where the Sun King seemed always to outshine even the most elaborate spectacle he could engineer. The scene also evokes the theatricality inherent in the experience of watching actual battles, for centuries a common European practice. Before technological innovations such as rifles, long-range artillery, and airpower dramatically expanded the battlespace, spectators could with a reasonable expectation of safety attend a battle in progress as if it were a kind of theater. The phenomenon finds literary expression in the twelfth-century *Poem of the Cid* when, in the second cantar, Rodrigo escorts his wife and daughters to a fortress tower in Valencia so that they can watch him in action: "I shall take up arms to meet this attack, and my wife and daughters shall see me fight and behold with their eyes how we earn our bread," writes the anonymous poet of the epic, translated here by Rita Hamilton and Janet Perry. "Stay in this part of the castle, wife," orders the hero, "and do not be afraid when you see me fight."

History is replete with accounts of spectators—military as well as civilian—observing battles as they unfold. At the beginning of the nineteenth century, the Duke of Wellington complained to a correspondent that battle had become the ultimate tourist attraction and that each eyewitness tended to be as unreliable as the next: "The truth regarding the battle of Waterloo is this," he informed the Earl of Clancarty: "there exists in England an insatiable curiosity upon every subject which has occasioned a *mania* for traveling and for writing. The battle of Waterloo having been fought within reach, every creature who could afford it traveled to view the field; and almost everyone who came who could write, wrote an account." He added sardonically, "It is very doubtful whether I was present in the battle of Waterloo."

In *The Mask of Command* (1987) the military historian John Keegan adduces this letter and others as evidence of Wellington's "caustic skepticism about the possibility of ordering visual impressions in a valid version of events." At Waterloo, Wellington surveyed the field from the high ground, but he also rode into the midst of the battle when he deemed it necessary, on occasion finding himself perhaps as close as fifty yards to the enemy. As Keegan explains, a commander like Wellington based decisions on visual observation but also—when his view was obscured by smoke, fog, or terrain—on sound. The advent of the rifle later in the century pushed generals farther back and "made Wellington's habits of exposure suicidal." As late as the American Civil War, however, "it was still just possible for a general . . . to ride about his line while his army was in action." A magnificent horseman like Ulysses S. Grant, for example, could manage a battlefront several miles long and thus found it feasible to command in the style of his hero, Zachary Taylor, who, as Grant notes in his memoirs, "saw for himself, and gave orders to meet the emergency" of the moment during the Mexican War just over a decade before.

As Keegan documents, the massive expansion of armies and fronts in the early twentieth century—the most dramatic example is

118 • RARITAN ON WAR

the Western Front of World War I, which stretched for hundreds of miles—changed the relationship of commanders to the battles they directed and created all those chateau-generals working from headquarters often far behind the lines. The use of airpower, especially long-range bombing, in World War II exponentially enlarged the geography of combat. This trend toward expansion continues today with the use of Predator drones remotely controlled from thousands of miles away. Yet even as the physical distance between decision makers and battles has grown, innovations in technology have brought more images of war closer than ever for combatants in the fight, for military and political leaders observing from remote headquarters, and for civilian spectators at home.

Video intelligence has obvious tactical significance. The U.S. Army, for example, has fielded new technologies by means of which helicopter pilots in the air and soldiers on the ground can receive direct video feeds from unmanned surveillance aircraft. The real-time digital feed also theoretically narrows the ever-widening distance between a battle and the commanders who watch it. Senior military and civilian leaders can now give orders while monitoring images of different engagements miles away rather than, as they did in previous eras, receiving and responding to news of troop movements, developing situations, or battles in progress by means of slower mechanisms, such as the runner, dispatch rider, telegraph, or field telephone. In some sense today's technology approximates the firsthand observation enjoyed by a Wellington or Grant, yet the high-tech medium potentially alters the dynamic of command and control by fostering the tantalizing illusion that it can yield perfect information—that the visual image trumps other evidence and that events can be seen and understood with a transparency and completeness unavailable to a participant in the thick of the fight.

There are putative operational advantages to being able to survey remote events: real-time video facilitates real-time decision making. In 1993, General William F. Garrison and his staff at the

Joint Operations Center in Somalia had unprecedented access to the sounds (relayed on multiple radio frequencies) and images (provided by observation helicopters and an Orion spy plane) of the disastrous raid on Mogadishu. Yet, as Mark Bowden explains in *Black Hawk Down* (1999), "Garrison and his staff probably had more instant information about this unfolding battle than any commanders in history, but there wasn't much they could do but watch and listen. So long as things stayed on course, any decisions would be made by the men in the fight." As Bowden notes, U.S. surveillance was inevitably incomplete: not even multiple cameras can see everything at once.

The flood of imagery they do relay presents a significant cognitive challenge to the viewer. We labor under an illusion, as recent scientific studies have demonstrated, that we are efficient media multitaskers able to process a surfeit of stimuli from unrelated sources. Experiments at Stanford University and elsewhere have revealed, on the contrary, that the most confident multitaskers are in fact the least effective: "They're suckers for irrelevancy," one researcher said of heavy multitaskers. "Everything distracts them." An army officer deployed to Afghanistan around the time of Operation Anaconda once described to me the dizzying sensation of watching multiple feeds simultaneously displayed on a giant screen at an airbase. He felt that he had to guard against being mesmerized by the images: events in one quadrant, he explained, could easily distract a viewer from something important going on elsewhere. It wasn't always easy to know either where to look or for how long. Decision making in such circumstances also can be compromised by the possibility that commanders, who must depend on faculties of reason and dispassionate equilibrium, may be unduly swayed by their heated emotional responses to dynamic real-time representations of violence.

Civilians share, though to a lesser degree, in this new proximity to the battlefield. But the stakes are different for ostensibly disinterested observers—for journalists and the rest of us who consume

120 • RARITAN ON WAR

the images they make available. Television is often credited with changing attitudes toward war on the American home front in the 1960s and 1970s by bringing images of Vietnam into the living room. But now, forty years on, the visual manifestations of war have multiplied and grown more complex. In any attempt to see America's wars in Iraq and Afghanistan, we are confronted by the competing perspectives of Al Jazeera abroad, various media outlets at home, and the special phenomenon of the embedded journalist, who, perhaps at the price of critical distance, brings noncombatants as close as they have ever been to the fight.

As Michael Ignatieff argued in the *New York Times Magazine* in 2004, videography has itself become a weapon in these wars: Osama Bin Laden's use of video messages; the taping of executions by al-Qaeda and other groups of forced confessions and decapitations (most memorably, that of Daniel Pearl); and the photographs of abused prisoners taken by guards at Abu Ghraib. Ignatieff proposes that "the terrorist as impresario" and "the torturer as video artist" are cooperatively engaged in the staging of a "new kind of reality show": "news editors still screen the worst moments out, but over the past twenty-five years . . . have spared us less and less." Ignatieff likens the effect of these images to that of pornography in their ability to make "audiences feel curious and aroused, despite themselves, then ashamed, possibly degraded and finally, perhaps, just indifferent." Imagery in the Iraq War, he suggests, "has replaced argument; indeed, atrocity footage has become its own argument. One horrendous picture seems not just to follow the other but also to justify it. From Abu Ghraib to decapitation footage and back again, we the audience are caught in a loop." Important questions about the legitimacy and necessity of the war have been submerged within what Ignatieff calls a "darkening vortex" of "barbarism."

Image has been argument in a sense since the beginning of the photographic age. When the Civil War photographer Mathew Brady exhibited "The Dead of Antietam" in a New York gallery in

October 1862, only weeks after the battle, the *Times* reported that the images did something the rolls of the dead in the newspapers never could: "Each of these little names that the printer struck off so lightly last night," the article explains, "represents a bleeding, mangled corpse. . . . There is nothing very terrible to us, however, in the list, though our sensations might be different if the newspaper carrier left the names on the battlefield and the bodies at our doors instead. . . . Mr. Brady has done something to bring home to us the terrible reality and earnestness of war. If he has not brought bodies and laid them in our dooryards and along the streets, he has done something very like it." Calling the photographs "weird copies of carnage," the *Times* reporter observed that they had "a terrible distinctness. By the aid of the magnifying glass, the very features of the slain may be distinguished." But what argument did spectators in the gallery take away from Brady's images? That war is terrible, certainly. That those who come face-to-face with its minutely detailed terror ought to bring it to an end, probably not. After the war was over, Americans apparently lost interest even in the first argument: Brady went bankrupt with his vast collection of war imagery.

Modern technology has brought "home" war's "terrible reality and earnestness" as never before. Yet high-definition video notwithstanding, we are as likely as those early nineteenth-century tourists Wellington condemned to get things wrong, even though the apparently unmediated, immediate fidelity of the images we consume may convince us of the infallibility of our perspective. Since the beginning of the recent wars in Iraq and Afghanistan, there has been no shortage of cameras attempting to instruct us on how to get it right—on the proper direction and duration of our gaze. Feature films about the war were for several years box-office poison in Hollywood, but documentaries have proliferated since the beginning. Some of those documentaries compel us to consider as much the problem of regarding war as the war itself. Jehane Noujaim's *Control Room* (2004), for instance, presents Al Jazeera's alternative

122 • RARITAN ON WAR

view to the coverage of journalists embedded with U.S. and British forces. More recently, in *Restrepo* (2010), Sebastian Junger and the late Tim Hetherington opened a window onto a unit deployed to a remote combat outpost in Afghanistan's Korengal Valley. Hetherington and Junger shot the footage themselves with handheld cameras. The director Deborah Scranton, presented several years ago with an opportunity to embed in Iraq, tried a different approach. She gave digital cameras to several members of a New Hampshire National Guard unit, who carried them in camp and on patrols, sometimes attaching them to their vehicles. The resulting film, *The War Tapes*, won Best International Documentary at the 2006 Tribeca Film Festival.

The War Tapes brings us as close as possible to the soldier's-eye view of war; it is, among other things, an exercise in sympathetic identification. As such, it exemplifies the media's corrective emphasis in the wake of Vietnam on distinguishing soldiers from the causes for which their government sends them to fight. Scranton has explained that her filmmaking is inspired by the "living journalism" of James Agee and Walker Evans. "If war negates humanity," she has explained, "then film—maybe especially film that shows war from the inside—can ensure that even when we fight, we hold on to and bear witness to our humanity. We found a way in this film to smash through that wall. We found the possibility of empathy in the middle of war." Scranton here accords film extraordinary, perhaps transcendent, power. Beginning with the problematic premise that "war negates humanity"—one could just as easily argue that war defines humanity, so fundamental has it been to every stage in the history of civilization—she invests the camera with the capacity to restore that humanity by "bear[ing] witness . . . from the inside" for all those on the outside and by "evok[ing] empathy" in her largely civilian home-front audience for the soldiers who are the film's subject. But can a camera control the empathy it evokes? Scranton does not address the possibility that her film's images might also arouse empathy for the civilians caught in the war zone or even for the enemy. And what, exactly, is the audience expected to do with the empathy that has been elicited?

The audience with which I watched Scranton's film at the festival and the critics who rewarded it underwent what Susan Sontag described in *Regarding the Pain of Others* (2003)—a book largely motivated by the Iraq War—as "a quintessential modern experience": "Being a spectator of calamities taking place in another country." This marks a radical shift from a prephotographic age, in which various theorists confronted the challenge of making the invisible real and thereby generating empathy for calamities unseen. In the 1780s, Edmund Burke called attention to a principle of "geographical morality" that permitted Britons to ignore the unseen abuses perpetrated by their countrymen on the other side of the world in India. Several decades before, Adam Smith in *The Theory of Moral Sentiments* (1759) considered how "a man of humanity in Europe . . . would be affected" on hearing that "the great empire of China, with all its myriads of inhabitants, was suddenly swallowed up by an earthquake." Smith carefully traces the various stages through which this hypothetical "man of humanity" would pass: expressions of sorrow; philosophical reflections on the "precariousness of human life"; calculations about the commercial and political effects of the disaster; and, finally, the resumption of "his business or his pleasure . . . with the same ease and tranquillity, as if no such accident had happened."

Smith's argument is that news of distant suffering—news that does not concern us in a manifestly personal way—can excite only "passive feelings," which "are almost always . . . sordid and . . . selfish." If the humane European were "to lose his little finger tomorrow," Smith concludes, "he would not sleep to-night; but, *provided he never saw them*, he will snore with the most profound security over the ruin of a hundred millions of his brethren, and the destruction of that immense multitude seems plainly an object less interesting to him, than this paltry misfortune of his own" (emphasis added). Social and political justice, which often requires

124 · RARITAN ON WAR

the valuing of unseen strangers, depends for Smith on the individual's ability to see with "the eye of" an "impartial spectator" and thus to correct the "natural misrepresentations of self-love" that turn us inward. Smith's caveat, "provided he never saw them," insists on the efficacy of visual witness as a sympathetic conduit as well as the vital importance, especially in a prephotographic age when so much suffering necessarily went unseen, of a successfully functioning moral imagination that can empathize with suffering it cannot see. In the age of the moving image, the imaginative faculty further atrophies: as the film critic David Thomson reminds us, films are even less "available to the imagination" than still photography. More and more evidence of human suffering becomes visible. The once clear distinctions between proximity and distance have been confused, the principle of geographical morality ostensibly replaced by a global one.

Yet the issue of whether the fellow feeling generated by the act of witnessing produces a corresponding response—protest or intervention—remains unsettled. Arguments about the value of sympathy tend to be imprecise in articulating how feeling is translated into action. In *The Fable of the Bees* (1714), Bernard Mandeville offered a thought experiment, much admired by Rousseau, that strikes at the heart of the problem. Mandeville writes of an agonized prisoner locked in a cell and forced to watch a wild animal mutilate a child just beyond his reach. The impotence of the distraught prisoner animates Mandeville's suggestion that even a highwayman, housebreaker, or murderer "could feel Anxieties on such an Occasion," as well as his conclusion: the ability to be moved by such a spectacle demands no particular virtue or self-denial. This argument suggests the very real possibility that sympathy, even when it is provoked on location in the eyewitness, does not naturally lead to action.

Sontag addresses the issue in *Regarding the Pain of Others* by suggesting that the two most influential (and opposed) theories about the impact of photography in our age—that moral response to atrocity is "mobilized by images" and that the glut of imagery has dulled our moral sense—have almost reached "the stature of platitudes." Sontag, whose own understanding of the work of the image continued to evolve, wondered whether we are paralyzed or provoked by the "culture of spectatorship." "Could one," she asks, "be mobilized actively to oppose war by an image (or a group of images)?" That's the story we like to tell ourselves about photojournalism in Vietnam: about Nick Ut's 1972 photo of children fleeing a napalm strike, for example, or John Laurence's televised reports from the battlefield. But the outrage produced by imagery is invariably short- lived, as the response to Brady's Antietam photos illustrated. "For a long time," writes Sontag, "people believed that if the horror could be made vivid enough, most people would finally take in the outrageousness, the insanity of war." If the photographic image has not yet called a halt to war, it seems unlikely that further technological innovation will achieve that end. Yet we persist in an often naive celebration of the camera's (especially the video camera's) ability to elicit a meaningful response to the violent confusion of war. We are still governed by the idea that photographic documentation is a moral imperative.

Likening the history of battle to that of a ball, Wellington complained to one correspondent: "Some individuals may recall all the little events of which the great result is the battle won or lost; but no individual can recollect the order in which, or the exact moment at which they occurred, which makes all the difference as to their value or importance." The photographic record replaces memory's inaccurate reconstruction of events with an editorial reconstruction, the technical virtuosity of which seduces us into believing its veracity. How much closer, the camera demands, would we like to get? It plunges us into the aesthetic and moral ambiguities of reconstructing reality through the lens of a manufactured authenticity. Sometimes the illusion is created by the transparency of the medium: the fidelity of the sound, the photographic clarity of the image, and the so-called invisible cutting characteristic of

126 · RARITAN ON WAR

the classic Hollywood style of editing. There is a contrasting school of filmmaking, however, of which the Italian neorealists and later the members of the French New Wave were perhaps the most influential practitioners, that emphasized the imperfections of the medium and capitalized on the power of the camera to interrupt the illusion.

One of the most provocative explorations of the latter style of filmmaking is Gillo Pontecorvo's *The Battle of Algiers* (1966), a film that raises important suspicions about its own medium and that has become one of cinema's reigning allegories of counterinsurgency, the dominant mode of contemporary warfare. A Pentagon screening organized by the Directorate for Special Operations and Low-Intensity Conflict in the summer of 2003 helped to spark a resurgence of interest in Pontecorvo's film, which had languished since the late 1960s, when various radical groups such as the Black Panthers and the Palestine Liberation Organization considered it a handbook of revolutionary violence. For the Algerians themselves, who contributed financially and personally to the film's making, it has remained a seminal expression of colonial resistance.

David Ignatius, who reported on the Pentagon screening in the *Washington Post*, regarded the event as "a hopeful sign that the military is thinking creatively and unconventionally about Iraq." About a week later, Michael T. Kaufman, writing in the *New York Times*, quoted a Pentagon official as saying, "The film offers historical insight into the conduct of French operations in Algeria, and [the screening] was intended to prompt informative discussion of the challenges faced by the French." The flier announcing the event read: "How to win a battle against terrorism and lose the war of ideas. Children shoot soldiers at point-blank range. Women plant bombs in cafes. Soon the entire Arab population builds to a mad fervor. Sound familiar? The French have a plan. It succeeds tactically, but fails strategically. To understand why, come to a rare showing of this film." Back in 2003, a showing of Pontecorvo's film was indeed "rare." More recently, screened by at least some civilian and military leaders, championed by many educators, referred to in various venues as a cautionary tale about imperial brutality or about the near impossibility of winning a counterinsurgency, *The Battle of Algiers* seems to be everywhere. Its ubiquity has a great deal to do with a successful marketing campaign. The film has been refreshed in a newly struck 35mm print. It was remastered, repackaged, and recontextualized in a three-DVD set released by the Criterion Collection in 2004, which includes an array of special features. In addition to several documentaries containing interviews with Pontecorvo himself and with others who participated in the actual events or in the making of the film (or both), there are contemporary reflections by filmmakers as well as by the counterterrorism experts Richard A. Clarke and Michael A. Sheehan, who propose that the real lesson of the film is, in Clarke's words, that "terrorism works" in the absence of a political strategy to combat it. Local policing and counterinsurgency victories will come to nothing unless, Clarke explains in a phrase that echoes the Vietnam-era formulation about "hearts and minds," we can win "the battle of ideas and values."

Yet Pontecorvo's film offers no viable solution to that pressing problem. Skeptical of the film's applicability to the current conflict, Charles Paul Freund pointed out in an article in *Slate* that the film's "lessons . . . are a lot more ambiguous than this Pentagon blurb implies." Freund notes that it is on the subject of torture that *The Battle of Algiers* "is potentially the most valuable and most dangerous as a point of comparison for the US military," because of the film's message "that torture is an efficient countermeasure to terror," a message we know to be at once morally repugnant and pragmatically false. Another revelation of the film might be, as David Thomson suggests, the ruinous stupidity that overtakes "armies when they do not have political control of their work."

One underlying cause of the film's resurrection is the comfort of analogy. "Though analogy is often misleading," Samuel Butler once wrote, "it is the least misleading thing we have." When things

128 · RARITAN ON WAR

go well, imagining we have outstripped the past, we call attention to our own exceptionalism. But analogies always return with a vengeance in less stable times, and nothing attracts analogists like a crisis. Even those cataclysms—the events of 11 September 2001—we regard as unprecedented are feverishly measured against other cataclysms we once thought unique—the events of 7 December 1941. When Harold Clurman saw *The Battle of Algiers* at the New York Film Festival at Lincoln Center in 1967, members of the audience made analogies to Vietnam, Newark, Detroit, and Watts. The French paratroopers who found themselves in Algeria after fighting in Indochina used to call the Algerians "Viets." The festival audience and the paratroopers got it wrong, and the current analogies may, Freund contends, be just as dubious. France's situation—130 years of colonial rule, its comparative proximity to its colony, the determination of the *pieds-noirs*—created a totally different dynamic from that faced by the United States in Iraq or Afghanistan.

Nevertheless, the fact that the current battle against Islamic jihadism is a driving force behind the film's popularity—explicitly the raison d'être for the Criterion release—obliges its champions to insist on the validity of the analogy in their analyses of the film. The documentary *Five Directors* (included in the Criterion package) contains a number of such comparisons. Julian Schnabel, for example, claims that the film feels like "black and white" news from Iraq; it is, he opines, the "same thing." Oliver Stone, similarly insistent that the film is a "relevant" and "resonant" parable of oppression, calls particular attention to the Algerian bombers' willingness "to die" for their cause. Spike Lee, recognizing the film's nuances, returns to a conclusion others have drawn over the years when he calls the French paratroopers' torture of the Algerians and the Gestapo's treatment of the French Resistance the "same thing." For his part, Richard Clarke is "happy" to speculate that al-Qaeda has seen the film because it has adopted the technique of exploding bombs simultaneously in multiple locations.

This preoccupation with paralleling historical moments short-changes the question of what it means for this film to have become such an important reference for policymakers as well as for a broader audience, but it has also obscured the film's contribution to our thinking about the viability of another kind of problem, one central to film theory since its beginnings—the ability of cinema accurately to represent the reality of war. Pontecorvo himself, skeptical of the film's political value, observed not long before his death in 2006, "The most that *The Battle of Algiers* can do is teach how to make cinema, not war." One of the things the documentary style of Pontecorvo's film can show us is that the greater the appearance of authenticity and the more profound and complete the artificiality, the more exquisite the deception.

Consider, for example, the claim made by veterans of World War II that the opening scenes of the D-Day landings in Steven Spielberg's *Saving Private Ryan* (1998) were the most realistic ever achieved on film. "It couldn't be more real," said one on *The NewsHour with Jim Lehrer*; "It was a very real experience," offered another. Spielberg declared his intention "to approximate the look and the smells of what battle and combat is really like." He and his cinematographer, Janusz Kaminski, achieved their goal by electing not to storyboard the scene, and by using a handheld camera and running the film through a desaturation process that would reproduce the bleached-out look of a 1940s color newsreel. For Paul Fussell, the film's value lies in its willingness to show what other films have not: "In war films you don't often see arterial blood pumping out." But it is a trick of the eye that makes Saving Private Ryan more authentic than a documentary or, for that matter, than those films about World War II from the 1940s that contain actual footage. The feature-film directors Frank Capra, John Huston, John Ford, George Stevens, and William Wyler all filmed actual battles for the Armed Services. Many subsequently incorporated that footage into fiction films: Ford's *Sands of Iwo Jima* (1949) is a representative example. If Spielberg's film appears, in the opinion of those

130 · RARITAN ON WAR

who actually participated in the D-Day landing, to achieve something more realistic than earlier films, it vindicates the film theorist Siegfried Kracauer's insistence that "life photographed"—the documentary or newsreel, for example—"is not necessarily synonymous with the image of life."

Pontecorvo's achievement is subtler than Spielberg's because it sticks to one register, while Spielberg resorts to the frame story of the Ryan family reunion at a Normandy cemetery, which is pure Hollywood in both look and message. *The Battle of Algiers* achieves its reality effect by using all of the technological tools at its disposal to make itself appear less technologically sophisticated and more like a documentary newsreel. The film earns its realist stripes by appearing to be stripped of all artistic amplification. Pontecorvo's interest was in producing what he called "a stolen record of historical events." *Reportage! Reportage!* was the directorial mantra that governed life on the set. Nevertheless, *The Battle of Algiers* was not an experiment along the lines of those eighteenth-century fictions that masqueraded as "true histories." It wasn't intended to fool anyone. In the United States the film originally ran with a disclaimer that avowed fiction rather than fact: "Not one foot of newsreel or documentary film has been used." Depending on the print one screens, this disclaimer may or may not appear, but it served as a kind of boast—as if to say, *Look how real it all seems!*

How, then, did Pontecorvo achieve what A. O. Scott has called "the impression that history is not being reconstructed but rather witnessed"? For one, he was indebted to the Italian neorealist tradition, especially to the films of Roberto Rossellini. In *Paisan* (1946)—a film Pontecorvo described as moving because it was "so real . . . so clear and precise"—and in *Rome, Open City* (1945), Rossellini's technique arose as much from circumstance as from ideology: whatever subsequent theorists wish to say about the neorealist camera as democratic instrument, the grainy newsreel quality of Rossellini's film is an effect of the inferior black-market film stock available in occupied Rome. In addition, Rossellini used footage—filmed covertly—of marching German soldiers at the beginning of the film, taking advantage of history passing before his eyes.

Rossellini's style arose organically from circumstance. Pontecorvo, working belatedly—twenty years after *Open City* and almost a decade after the battle in the Casbah that his own film depicts—had to go to far greater lengths to contrive the neorealist look that had become the stamp of truth and authenticity. Sontag suggests that the appearance of "artistry" compromises "the photography of atrocity" for many contemporary spectators. Pontecorvo's artistry worked to conceal itself: he achieved the grainy, high-contrast production values associated with the documentary genre through patient and sophisticated technique, including an internegative process. In *Algiers* we have the painstakingly orchestrated simulation of what Sontag calls "anti-art" style: "impartiality and truthfulness," Pontecorvo insisted, were "the DNA of film." Dismayed with the rough cut, which had the continuity editing typical of the Hollywood style, Pontecorvo found a new editor who achieved a "sense of truth" more important than conventions through the more disruptive juxtaposition of images. Parts of the film display rather conventional editing: the cutting is perhaps most obtrusive in the scenes of armed conflict. As an embodiment of a "sense of truth," the resulting film is nevertheless more calculated and consistent than *Open City*, which actually disrupts its neorealistic depictions of the Italians with camp portrayals of the German SS Major Bergmann and his predatory associate, Ingrid, who leer and ogle like silent movie villains.

The score of *The Battle of Algiers* was as strategically arranged as its images. After hearing the music for Sergio Leone's *For a Few Dollars More* (1965), Pontecorvo hired Ennio Morricone to score his film. Pontecorvo and Morricone's collaboration was precise. One example that especially pleased Pontecorvo: the same Bach-like theme accompanies images of French and Algerian dead in order to elicit the same affective response. Pontecorvo did not wish

132 • RARITAN ON WAR

to legislate our sympathies but to complicate our experience by forcing us to confront the dead on both sides.

Photographs, Major Bergmann claims in one of *Open City's* self-conscious allusions to the function of the image, permit him to stroll through Rome every night in search of his enemies without ever leaving his office. In *The Battle of Algiers* the French police commissioner also collects and reviews photographs of his adversaries. Pontecorvo does not allow him a Rossellini-like wink at the audience, but he does permit the French colonel Mathieu, in the context of a briefing to his paratroopers, to call attention to the medium. Mathieu screens for his men the police surveillance films taken of checkpoints around the Casbah. The critic Stuart Klawans suggests that the message of this scene is that "film is unreliable." Mathieu points out the fallibility of the cameraman's "hunch." The cameraman, distracted by the irrelevant detail, fails to discover the terrorists. But in fact the footage proves the unreliability not of film but of police methods, methods the French Army will soon replace with a definitive search-and-destroy campaign. The cameraman was a faithful recorder. His lens did nothing but follow the inclinations of the guards rather than his own; his camera simply traced their suspicions and lapses in concentration.

The effectiveness of Pontecorvo's film depends on the illusion that he, like the police cameraman, is simply recording the chronicle of Algerian liberation—following history's path wherever it leads. Pontecorvo referred to his aesthetic as "the dictatorship of truth." His approach resulted in a more nuanced film than the one Saadi Yacef, former leader of National Liberation Front (FLN) operations in the Casbah and the man instrumental in getting the film made, originally proposed. Pontecorvo and his collaborator Franco Solinas dismissed Yacef's screenplay, based on his memoir, as propaganda: a "laudatory pamphlet about their rebellion." Yacef insists that his memoirs could be written in "the language of cinema," but part of what Pontecorvo seems to have meant by

ELIZABETH D. SAMET · 133

cinematic "truth" is balance: he wanted to "get inside the minds of both sides." He believed that both sides "do horrendous things . . . in battle," no matter where justice lies, and he hoped to acknowledge French "motives" even as he condemned French methods. The paratroopers were not, for him, "monsters." Resisting the hovering analogy, he insisted that they were not the SS.

Pontecorvo's treatment of his actors was also vital to achieving what he termed the "feeling" or "smell" of truth. Obsessed with finding the face that corresponded to his imagining of each character, Pontecorvo searched long and hard to assemble his cast of nonactors. Once assembled, they were subjected to Pontecorvo's demanding direction. Describing the director's penchant for multiple takes—fifty in the case of one shot—Jean Martin, the film's lone professional actor, who plays Colonel Mathieu, reports that by the final take he was so tired that he had no control left. Martin notes that the Algerians seemed actually to be reliving the events that had happened several years before, a point echoed by Pontecorvo in his claim that his nonactors were not acting at all— that the camera had been forgotten as they relived their own histories. Many of the Algerians who appeared in the film had taken part in the actual conflict; others, such as Zohra Drif-Bitat, refused to participate in its re-creation. (Drif-Bitat planted the bomb in the Milk Bar, an event depicted in the film.) In another example of Pontecorvo's theory of acting, the man he chose to play Ali La Pointe, a thief politicized in prison, was himself a petty criminal.

No one was more important to *The Battle of Algiers* than Saadi Yacef, who appears in the film with a new name in an old role. Yacef claims that the only thing he knew about movies was Julien Duvivier's *Pépé le Moko* (1937), certain scenes of which had been shot in the Casbah and in which Yacef had been asked to be an extra. Yacef's interviews reveal his proprietary attitude toward Pontecorvo's film, which he clearly regarded as a kind of vindication. He asserts ownership of both the film's physical location—he

134 · RARITAN ON WAR

boasts about rebuilding exploded parts of the Casbah so that they could be blown up all over again on film—as well as of the experience depicted. Pontecorvo, he claims at one point, simply reproduced his actions. "It was difficult to play myself," he admits. "But in the film, it became a game in which I let myself be guided and directed." Yacef's submission to direction was not always easy: once, after one too many takes, he asked Pontecorvo, "Are you trying to kill me?"

Although, like the French director Robert Bresson, Pontecorvo used nonactors, his realism is never accidental. By contrast, Bresson courted "accidental occurrences" and "impediments." "What I disapprove of," he told an interviewer, "is photographing . . . things that are not real. Sets and actors are not real." The torture scenes in *The Battle of Algiers* would have been unthinkable in a Bresson film. In *A Man Escaped* (1956), for instance, the director refused to show the beating of a prisoner: "The audience knows that the actor isn't really being beaten," Bresson explained, "and such falsity would stop the film." This is a world away from the sort of reality effect attempted in *The Battle of Algiers*.

Julien Duvivier's *Pépé le Moko*, that other Casbah film so compelling to American audiences that it was remade practically shot-for-shot in Hollywood as *Algiers* (1938), has one detail—an error, actually—that marks it out as in one sense the direct antithesis of *The Battle of Algiers*. Jean Gabin, the great French star who plays Pépé, happened to be wearing his own shirt while filming a particular scene in a café. At one point his suit jacket flies open to reveal the monogram "JG" on his shirt pocket. Pontecorvo would never have allowed this gaffe to remain in the final cut, disrupting the illusion, calling accidental attention to and thus reinforcing the film's fictionality.

If *Pépé* stands as an example of unabashed illusion, Pontecorvo's film embodies the duplicitousness of reality. After the first New York screening in 1967, Clurman called *The Battle of Algiers* "a masterpiece of epic realism" in the *Nation*. "From the specialist's point of view," he wrote, "this film is remarkable for being an entirely convincing 'documentary' of which not one foot is composed of stock shots or newsreel material. Yet one finds that one is *there* in the midst of the moment. A sense of the actual is never compromised by the taint of contrivance for effect." The genius of the deception—my term, not Clurman's—is that Pontecorvo's crowd scenes managed to "convey reality more strikingly than do the techniques of cinema verité" itself. One measure of the film's perceived authenticity—or at least its authentic cultural and political impact—was the fact that it was not shown in Paris until 1971. After it won the 1966 Golden Lion at Venice, the French delegation walked out, threatening reprisals against Italian film. In Algiers, there was another bizarre testament to the film's verisimilitude. When one faction of the FLN "surrounded another with tanks and ousted it from power," according to Freund, witnesses "literally thought that another scene" for Pontecorvo's film was being shot.

The supposed permeability between film and real life in *The Battle of Algiers* evokes a pale reflection of cinema's originary myth. The so-called train effect reputedly occurred when members of the earliest film audiences at the turn of the twentieth century, confronted by the onscreen image of a train arriving in a station, horses stampeding, or some other action moving toward the camera, fainted or ran in terror for the doors. The film theorist Christian Metz has suggested that this myth was cultivated by subsequent generations of filmgoers in order to highlight their own sophistication by attributing a childlike "credulity" to the spectators of earlier days.

One of the most compelling aspects of seeing *The Battle of Algiers* for the first time—and preferably that first screening is unaccompanied by the disclaimer that gives up the game—is that one is never sure what one is watching: documentary or fiction. In this way the film pits our own nostalgia for childlike credulity against a savvy self-awareness consistent with the postmodern experience. It would be a mistake, however, to conflate the experience even of

136 · RARITAN ON WAR

modern theater with the cinema or to assume that they could work the same effect on their respective audiences. Metz calls attention to a fundamental difference in the two art forms in *The Imaginary Signifier* (1977): "At the theater, Sarah Bernhardt may tell me she is Phèdre or, if the play were from another period and rejected the figurative regime, she might say, as in a type of modern theatre, that she is Sarah Bernhardt. But at any rate, I should see Sarah Bernhardt. At the cinema, she could make the same two kinds of speeches too, but it would be her shadow that would be offering them to me (or she would be offering them in her own absence). Every film is a fiction film." In our current rage for the technologically finessed approximation of reality, we find ourselves in a kind of second childhood with regard to the moving picture. We are so taken with the excellence and robustness of the facsimile that we are in danger of forgetting Metz's injunction, "Every film is a fiction film," its subjects merely chemically or electronically re-created shadows of themselves. The more we convince ourselves that we have an unparalleled facility with visual media, the more deeply we fall in love with our ability to reproduce the real with unprecedented fidelity—be it reality television or the documentary—the less scrupulously we interrogate what it means to be convinced of the reality of any given image, of what it means to take *The Battle of Algiers* for the thing itself.

At the press conference depicted in *The Battle of Algiers*, amid the still photographers' flashes and the hum of portable movie cameras, a reporter asks the captured FLN leader Larbi Ben M'Hidi whether he really thinks the Algerians have a chance against the superior firepower of the French. Ben M'Hidi replies that the FLN has a better chance than do the French of altering the course of history because their movement is rooted in an awakening popular insurgency that can overcome technological superiority. Mathieu then ends the conference before it has an effect contrary to its intent. His view of history is different from Ben M'Hidi's. At one point he even tells the press that the outcome of the struggle, which depends on "political will," is in the hands of reporters, not soldiers. His claim has become a commonplace complaint on the political right, that the media can lose, or bring an end to, a war by representing it in a particular way. At the same time, as the antiwar left complains, media can start or sustain wars by representing them in particular ways.

Mathieu's endorsement of the image's capacity to energize political will goes further than Pontecorvo's own aesthetic, described as a "dictatorship of truth." As the director himself contended, his film may teach us "how to make cinema" but not how to make—or, by extension, to end—war. There is an inherent gullibility in the enthusiasm for Pontecorvo's film as a repository of tactical, strategic, or political lessons. Instead, perhaps what the film reveals most clearly is the precarious relationship between art and sympathy. Politics may have animated Pontecorvo's decision to make the film, but his theory of filmmaking disconnected the ultimate truth of the image from its political context. The effect of this disjuncture, one of film's greatest achievements, is its capacity to confuse and confound the viewer's sympathetic inclinations: we are compelled to see both sides as victims and perpetrators simultaneously. In this regard, Pontecorvo's most important cinematic ancestor may well be not Rossellini's *Open City*, but D. W. Griffith's *The Birth of a Nation* (1915). Yet Griffith's film pulls our sympathies where reason and humanity emphatically tell us they ought not go, while Pontecorvo manipulates us for different ends by revealing that the reconstruction of events can direct our sympathies in several directions at once.

Jean-Luc Godard once pointed out that "realism . . . is never exactly the same as reality, and in the cinema it is of necessity faked." It was Godard who, along with François Truffaut and other exponents of the French New Wave, pioneered the use of the jump cut and other stylistic devices that once seemed so novel to audiences inured to the Hollywood style. Today, however, even these initially disruptive maneuvers have themselves become clichés,

138 · RARITAN ON WAR

the naturalized rhythms of cinema. Some commentators think it strange that Pontecorvo earned his living by making commercials, but the impulse seems consistent with an understanding of the supreme level of fakery required to achieve apparent authenticity. If Pontecorvo is right, and his film can teach something about "cinema, not war," then perhaps part of what it teaches is that cinema, while not impermeable to history, can regulate its temporal and spatial dislocations most completely through the dictatorship of verisimilitude. Lived experience and performance may bleed into one another—as in the case of Saadi Yacef—but Pontecorvo's brand of realism directs and regulates the flow. *The Battle of Algiers* may look realistic, but it is as constructed and stylized as *The Cabinet of Dr. Caligari* (1920). Even as we contemplate the prospect of an ever-expanding battlespace, a war without borders and without end, technology has made war seem more than ever like a theatrical pageant carefully staged for the instruction and delight of a vast audience of spectators made safe by geography, and often sensibility, from the spectacle they see.

The enthusiasm for and preoccupation with Pontecorvo's film as a vehicle for understanding counterinsurgency should not be confused with a serious scrutiny of the actual war before us. Interest in that less carefully scripted reality has waned noticeably even as the fervor for its "documentary" representation has grown. The "lesson" of Pontecorvo's film doesn't lie in the depiction of terrorist or counterinsurgent tactics or even in its closing scene's recognition of the ultimate victory of the insurgency. Rather, the film demonstrates the impotence of the spectator in the face of the image of things already done. The director Samuel Fuller, who knew real battles at first hand, declared in a cameo in one of Godard's films, "Film is like a battleground." His simile reminds us that the same smoke and fog that obscure the battle also enshroud the image of the battle no matter how definitive its resolution. Louis XIV intended the siege of Compiègne as "a demonstration of everything that happens in war." No image can give us that. The more preoccupied we become with the representation of war—the more willingly we surrender to the fidelity of war's digital reproduction of things done—the more easily do we both lose sight of the real event in progress and lose the ability to imagine the violence yet to be done.

Winter 2013

Mutabor: Halberstadt
KARL KIRCHWEY

I.

On Amtrak. The Connecticut shore scrolls past,
    stop-action frames from summer holidays:
    green coves, white beaches, bodies, spinnakers.
Where will I sit? One seat (it is the last).

An elderly woman with ash-gray hair
    prays the five decades of the rosary
    with her eyes closed and does not notice me.
I will be polite and brief with her.

I settle and take out a book of poems:
    no spiritualist, but at least I can read.
    She opens her eyes and slightly turns her head,
her face alert and kind. She says, "It seems

no one reads poetry on Amtrak these days"
    —an invitation, to which I respond that
    praying the rosary is also not
a pastime that one usually sees.

She smiles. And so we understand each other.
    It is enough. But then, as if to match
    what she has offered, on impulse I reach
inside my shirt for the *Rudraksha-mala*

KARL KIRCHWEY • 141

given me by my brother, one hundred eight
        five-faced beads plus one. She eyes them coolly
        as I say, "These are the tears of Rudra,
destroyer god and god of sorrow but

providing travelers a local calm:
        the dried seeds of a broad-leafed evergreen,
        worn on knotted crimson flax or cotton.
Rudra is also the god of holy wisdom."

Her gaze on me has now become ironic.
        "Ah, holy wisdom. Certainly we need
        such a fine thing. You've got your book to read,
and I'll get off before long in Norwalk,

but may I share a traveler's tale with you?"
        Uh-oh, I think, the Ancient Mariner
        has come to visit in the Quiet Car.
But it is much too late to change seats now.

II.

"April 8th, 1945 was a Sunday.
        We were in Halberstadt, Hungarian refugees
        fled from Berlin. The Germans hated us.
I was seven years old. I cannot easily

describe to you the meanness of that life:
        milk bottles filled with salt in the dairy window,
        mocking the plenty they pretended to;
the tobacconist's with empty carton on carton of

142 • RARITAN ON WAR

imported cigarettes and a sign that said
    Nur Attrappen, For Display Only;
    the poster VISIT MEDIEVAL GERMANY
satirical in ways unintended,

though American Express had closed long before.
    On its neglected storefront some boy's thumb
    had sketched out rudenesses I could not fathom
as I was hurried past them by my mother.

The cinemas, palaces of romance
    where I had looked away my infant sight,
    now played to empty houses every night,
having eliminated the saving distance

of fantasy for heaps of battle dead
    in newsreels, bombs descending from the skies,
    and as if closing off all futures but this,
even fortune-tellers had been outlawed.

Yet the seduction was more profound, really:
    jump-cuts and close-ups schooled my unarmed eye for
    the shock effects of life and total war.
I learned to see the world distractedly,

part of (it seemed) an invulnerable
    collective with those around me who watched
    what, like that dusty plate-glass window touched
with obscene shapes, lived in an archetypal

foreground of mere desire. I could not know
    what had been lost, which were the moral feelings
    connecting people and connecting things
behind the surface, its flicker and glow.

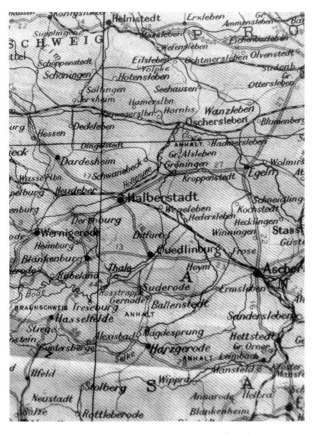

U.S. Army Air Force escape map detail:
Halberstadt, Germany (map printed on acetate rayon,
sewn into flight suit lining), 1944.

Arthur Cohen (1928–2012), graphite and charcoal drawing
(dated 30 November 1945) of
B-17 Flying Fortress during bombing raid.

III.

"But this was all background to April 8th.
　　Promptly at eleven o'clock that morning,
　　we heard the faraway drone approaching:
a wave of two hundred planes, a second wave

of more than a hundred, they laid down carpets
　　of high explosive and incendiary bombs
　　reducing all the world to jarring atoms
by their thud and tremor and bestial grunt that alternates

suction-pressure-suction-pressure, until
　　my parents told me that I must not breathe,
　　so that my lungs would not be torn. Dazed with
the noise, we simply cowered. A cathedral

of light rose in the streets, a wicked sound
　　like the devil laughing, or, as the fire
　　rose into hurricanes, a toccata
played on some monstrous organ. My mother's hand,

I held her hand and tried to think of a poem:
　　O tell me dear if I died before you did,
　　Would you weep and wrap me in my shroud?
I tried to think of Budapest, our home,

but nothing helped, and terror rustled like
　　wind in a thatched roof or a flock of birds,
　　as if a cauldron were over our heads
pouring down gasoline and rubber in a thick

Westendorf Post, Halberstadt, 8 April 1945.

KARL KIRCHWEY • 147

lava. My mother, in a rain-blue cape,
    told me that I must pray to the Virgin.
    I watched her fingers move through fifty-nine
beads and wished they were pasta in my soup,

for we had eaten nothing since the sixth.
    Be nice and good, I prayed to myself. Fold
    Your little hands. Pray to the Lord, my child.
The man whose Advent window had been dressed with

twelve thousand tin soldiers every year—
    the retreat from Moscow by Napoleon's army—
    was dead, along with his meticulous hobby,
his troops all reduced to a clot of solder.

The air was flurrying with burning pages:
    one fell on my wrist and briefly I read
    a text in negative before it shivered
to ash and mingled with a ubiquitous

new element, the mud of Halberstadt,
    compounded from plaster dust, shredded wallpaper,
    kilims and stained glass, ruptured human viscera,
splintered wood and fallen roofs of slate.

We hunched forward and gagged. Crowned with blue flame,
    what looked like tailor's dummies at grotesque angles
    lay in the street; or else they were fried eels.
My mother could not save me from the sight of them.

Around me I could hear it start already,
    the struggle to control the narrative
    by all those who had managed to survive,
regret and reason mingled with self-pity,

148 • RARITAN ON WAR

rising from devastation's stony rubbish
    even while, buried stories deep beneath,
    fire gnawed and rodents moved with avid stealth;
stolid and cunning in their stubborn wish,

those voices, mild, always exonerating,
    the useless adjectives, the airbrushed pronoun—
    On that terrible day they razed our beautiful town—
voices that accepted nothing and learned nothing.

Just once, as we left the city, I looked back:
    a German with a pushcart was trying to sell
    narcissus (for it was spring, after all)
beside a smoking mound of shattered brick."

IV.

A musing silence follows, though it is
    no respite, but like an attempt to damp
    what mutters and breathes, in its glowing sump,
behind the creosote-smeared furnace glass.

In it, I find a page has drifted past
    in my own mind, written in dented loops,
    part Palmer method, part unconfessed hopes,
my grandmother's, on which she kept a list

of raids my father flew over Germany
    in heavy bombers, that spring of '45,
    city by city, till he came home alive.
Once I could recite them all from memory,

Martini-Plan, Halberstadt, 8 April 1945.

150 • RARITAN ON WAR

places I've never been and do not know:
  Bitburg, Koblenz, Magdeburg, Zweibrücken,
  Siegen, Soest, Witzlar and Jungen
(I start to work the silent roll call through)

Dülwen, Rechlin, Reisholz, Castrop-Roxel,
  Bingen, Bebra . . . and no more. But was
  Halberstadt there, in that meticulous
hand, in which case—? I cannot recall—

But certain things my father said come back:
  the plane beside him that simply exploded
  and he thought, *It's like a movie, my God*;
the nightmare fighters, the dark blooms of flak;

the sleep from which he sometimes woke up screaming.
  Like working day shift in a factory,
  he said: expensive goods for immediate delivery.
His mind was an exhausted neutral thing

out of which he wrote letters home to please
  send pipe tobacco, salted nuts, fruitcake,
  that calf-bound ottavo of William Blake,
rubbers to fit size 10-c GI shoes. . . .

V.

"A man that Sunday had a movie camera"
  (her voice moves patiently toward its own doom),
  "and recorded the raid, although the film
could only have been processed in Dessau

Left: Standing, Staff Sergeant George W. Kirchwey (1920–1988) and fellow crew members in front of B-24 Liberator *BTO* (*Big Time Operator*), Attleborough, England, spring 1945.

Right: At the entrance to airbase for 734 Squadron, 453 Bombardment Group (H), Attleborough, England, spring 1945.

152 • RARITAN ON WAR

at a plant that was long since rubble.
  He wanted incontrovertible evidence
  of what had happened, but there was none, since
after all, the whirr and clatter of sequential

frames could only mimic jagged glimpses
  produced by trauma, personal memory,
  in such destruction, replacing history,
the past become forever discontinuous,

as survivors staggered onward, dazed or wild,
  with suitcases containing precious relics
  of ordinary life, the clothes and keepsakes
(in one, the shrunken corpse of a burned child):

so that it was not death—not death alone—
  that finally seemed hardest to forgive,
  but being doomed from now on to live
in broken fragments, all connection broken."

And then silence. We jostled side by side
  as the train banked and slowed by the sea's edge
  where a white heron studied its own image,
the morning not yet past, the day ahead,

and I with no handkerchief, for pity,
  though the tears of hell had stained her cheeks, I saw.
  Nor could I even wet my hands with dew
to soothe the face I knew would pray for me.

KARL KIRCHWEY • 153

◆ ◆ ◆

NOTES AND SOURCES

II.

The section relies for its detail in part on the following journalistic accounts included in the two volumes of *Reporting World War II* (New York: Library of America, 1995): William Walton, "Now the Germans Are the Refugees" (describing the fall of Aachen, autumn 1944); and Howard K. Smith, "Valhalla in Transition" (Berlin, autumn 1941).

"Infant sight": cf. Elizabeth Bishop's poem "Over 2000 Illustrations and a Complete Concordance" (1955).

"The unarmed eye" appears in Walter Benjamin's 1936 essay translated by Harry Zohn as "The Work of Art in the Age of Mechanical Reproduction" in Benjamin's *Illuminations* (New York: Schocken Books, 1969), 223.

Benjamin also speaks of "distraction as a variant of social conduct" (238); the formal correspondence between the constant changes expressed by film and the experiential "shock effect" of modern life is explored more fully and clearly in the second version of Benjamin's essay as translated by Harry Zohn and Edmund Jephcott and available in *The Work of Art in the Age of Its Technological Reproducibility, and Other Writings on Media* (Cambridge, MA: Harvard University Press, 2008). This section of the poem also refers to ideas in Susan Sontag's *On Photography* (New York: Picador, 1977), 16–17.

III.

The section makes use of anecdotal and historical information contained in Alexander Kluge's *The Air Raid on Halberstadt on 8 April 1945* (New York: Seagull Books, 2014), translated by

154 • RARITAN ON WAR

Martin Chalmers. It is also informed by Miron Białoszewski's *A Memoir of the Warsaw Uprising* (New York: Review Books, 2014), translated by Madeline G. Levine.

The section uses details from Edward R. Murrow's "Can They Take It?" (the London Blitz, September 1940), Janet Flanner (Genêt), "Letter from Cologne" (March 1945), and Martha Gellhorn, "Das Deutsches Volk" (Cologne, April 1945), all in *Reporting World War II*, as well as from A. C. Grayling, *Among the Dead Cities: The History and Moral Legacy of the WW II Bombing of Civilians in Germany and Japan* (New York: Walker, 2006), who quotes W. G. Sebald about the firebombing of Hamburg during the Royal Air Force's Operation Gomorrah in July 1943 (18).

The section paraphrases Erika Papp Faber's translations of two poems: "At the End of September," by Sándor Petőfi (1823–1849), and "For My Son," by János Arany (1817–1882), in *A Sampler of Hungarian Poetry*, ed. and trans. Erika Papp Faber (Budapest: Romanika Kiadó, 2012).

Burning books are described by Dr. Kemal Bakaršić, librarian of the National Museum in Sarajevo (destroyed by Serbia on 25–26 August 1992), in Robert Bevan's *The Destruction of Memory: Architecture at War* (London: Reaktion Books, 2006), 37.

IV.

In the file of my father's wartime correspondence is the transcript (in English and German) of a U.S. propaganda broadcast in which he participated on 5 April 1945. He spoke of his next-to-last mission over Münster: "The city stretched like an empty shell. It looked completely devastated, bomb-shattered buildings and rubble in all directions. . . . Work like that is no pleasure. But it's a job that must be done, and will be done over and over again until the Nazis stop it themselves by surrender. Now it's over at Münster. And it's over at Kassel too . . ."

This section paraphrases information in Brendan Gill, "Young Man behind Plexiglass" (August 1944), in *Reporting World War II*, and also includes information from Kluge's *Air Raid on Halberstadt* and Grayling's *Among the Dead Cities*.

V.

In *The Destruction of Memory*, Bevan quotes the French historian Pierre Nora (1931–) to the effect that "memory is simply what was called 'history' in the past; the two have merged" (16). But long before, in his essay "History" (1841), Ralph Waldo Emerson had written, "All history becomes subjective; in other words, there is properly no history, only biography."

Summer 2021

Bourne over Baghdad
ROBERT WESTBROOK

JOHN DOS PASSOS offered perhaps the most memorable portrait of the cultural critic Randolph Bourne in his novel *1919*. "If any man has a ghost," Dos Passos wrote, "Bourne has a ghost, a tiny twisted unscared ghost in a black cloak hopping along the grimy old brick and brownstone streets still left in downtown New York, crying out in a shrill soundless giggle: *War is the health of the state.*"

Dead at thirty-one in the influenza pandemic of late 1918, Bourne was in the last months of his brief life an outcast from the community of progressive reform intellectuals that had once welcomed him as a most promising acolyte. His sin, "in the crazy spring of 1917," was to turn the withering irony of his limpid prose on the rush of most of this community to join the Great War: "for Progress Civilization Education Service, Buy a Liberty Bond, Strafe the Hun, Jail the Objectors."

Bourne disturbed the peace of John Dewey and other intellectuals supporting Woodrow Wilson's crusade to make the world safe for democracy, and they made him pay for it. As Dos Passos put it, "He resigned from *The New Republic*; only *The Seven Arts* had the nerve to publish his articles against the war. The backers of *The Seven Arts* took their money elsewhere; friends didn't like to be seen with Bourne, his father wrote him begging him not to disgrace the family name. The rainbowtinted future of reform democracy went pop like a pricked soapbubble." But his enemies could not still his spirit. The giggle of Bourne's ghost was less soundless than Dos Passos imagined. His specter stood beside critics of many of the American wars that followed World War I. Dwight Macdonald invoked his shade during World War II, as did Noam Chomsky and Christopher Lasch during the Vietnam War.

Bourne's name no longer carries the resonance it once did in the wider culture; one of his recent biographers has labeled him a "forgotten prophet." Occasionally, his apparition has appeared in debates over the war in Iraq—though rarely with anything like a full appreciation of Bourne's dissent from Wilsonian orthodoxy. But since so many, on the right and left alike, have justified the Iraq War in strikingly Wilsonian terms, it is perhaps worth looking more attentively than we yet have to the ghost of "this little sparrowlike man" as we consider their arguments.

Bourne's wartime attack on Dewey is often said to have marked a break with Dewey's philosophical pragmatism, which he had once enthusiastically shared, but it did not. Rather, Bourne demanded that Dewey and other progressive intellectuals provide him with a compelling pragmatist case for American intervention in the war— that is, a good argument that would demonstrate that war was an effective means to the democratic ends that they sought, and that he shared with them. When none was forthcoming, Bourne instead made a pragmatist case against intervention, one cast within the framework for ethical deliberation he had learned from Dewey. That is, he turned Dewey's own "logic of practical judgment" on the illogic of the judgments that Dewey made about the war.

Bourne's argument fell on deaf ears. But it was, nonetheless, a powerful one. In a brilliant article titled "The Collapse of American Strategy" published in August 1917, Bourne argued that, if the end for which the United States entered the war was, as Wilsonians claimed, the creation of an international order that would prevent the recurrence of world war, it was worth asking, if one was a pragmatist, how entering the war was to serve and, since that April, had served as a means to this end. The country entered the war in the face of the resumption of German submarine attacks, prowar progressives argued, not to ensure an Allied victory but to prevent a German victory and to secure a negotiated "peace without victory" that could serve as the basis of the international organization necessary to prevent future conflicts. At the time, Bourne said,

158 • RARITAN ON WAR

"realistic pacifists" like himself had argued for the use of naval force to keep the shipping lanes free, a policy of "armed neutrality" aimed directly at the submarine problem. If it was successful in rendering submarine warfare ineffectual, such a policy might have convinced the Germans that they could not win, while at the same time it might have preserved the possibility of a negotiated settlement mediated by the United States. By entering the war, the United States lost any leverage it may have had for securing "peace without victory" and, indeed, lifted the hopes of the Allies for *"la victoire intégrale,"* a "knockout blow" against the Germans. If American participation in the war was supposed to liberalize the war aims of the Allies, it had been a miserable failure. Instead, American war aims themselves had been transformed. The nation had been effectively enlisted on behalf of the reactionary goal of an Allied "peace with victory," and "American liberals who urged the nation to war are therefore suffering the humiliation of seeing their liberal strategy for peace transformed into a strategy for a prolonged war."

Devastating as Bourne's criticism of the strategy of the Wilson administration was, his essays were even more damning of the even greater shortsightedness of Dewey and other "left Wilsonian" intellectuals and "new-republicans" who hoped to turn Wilson's war to ends far more radical than any contemplated by Wilson, let alone Colonel House. Moved by Wilson's rhetoric, these progressives defended American intervention in the war on the grounds that it would provide a unique opportunity to reorganize the world into a radically democratic social order. "Industrial democracy is on the way," Dewey told a *New York World* reporter in July 1917. "The rule of the Workmen and the Soldiers will not be confined to Russia; it will spread through Europe; and this means that the domination of all upper classes, even of what we have been knowing as 'respectable society,' is at an end."

This was, to say the least, poor prophecy—the result not of the informed judgment that Dewey's ethics required but of what he himself called "footless desires." As Bourne said, "The 'liberals' who claim a realistic and pragmatic attitude in politics have disappointed us in setting up and then clinging wistfully to the belief that our war could get itself justified for an idealistic flavor, or at least for a world-renovating purpose. . . . If these realists had had time in the hurry and scuffle of events to turn their philosophy on themselves, they might have seen how thinly disguised a rationalization this was of their emotional undertow."

Beneath the hard-boiled exterior of prowar liberal intellectuals lay a soft center immune to realism and pragmatic argument. In their hearts, Bourne observed, these intellectuals were bound to the dream of "a war free from any taint of self-seeking, a war that will secure the triumph of democracy and internationalize the world." So obviously flawed were their rational arguments for such a war that in order to explain their position one had to say "it is not so much what they thought as how they felt" that mattered most. "War in the interests of democracy! This was almost the sum of their philosophy," Bourne marveled. "The primitive idea to which they regressed became almost insensibly translated into a craving for action."

The war, Bourne noted, did occasion a sharp emotional conflict as "our desire for peace strove with our desire for national responsibility in the world." But the latter won out, as intellectuals gave way to "the conviction that we were ordained as a nation to lead all erring brothers toward the light of liberty and democracy." For Bourne, this plunge into "an emotional bath of these old ideals" was appalling: "the reversion of senility to that republican childhood when we expected the whole world to copy our republican institutions."

❖ ❖ ❖

One cannot read Bourne's war essays today without being struck by their pertinence to the current war in Iraq. Once more we have been assailed by Wilsonian rhetoric from the White House, ever more so since the prewar claim of a threat to American national

160 · RARITAN ON WAR

security posed by Saddam Hussein's weapons of mass destruction has collapsed.

George W. Bush and others in his administration have, of course, sometimes tried to recast the war ex post facto as a war that was necessary because of Saddam Hussein's putative *plans* to rebuild his weapons program. Needless to say, this sort of argument, had it been made before the war, would have engendered a much greater reluctance on the part of American politicians and the public at large to go to war than the claim that Saddam was forging an alliance with al-Qaeda, had stockpiled massive quantities of chemical and biological weapons, and was restarting his nuclear program. If claims about Saddam's future intentions had been thought a sufficient sales pitch for war, the administration would not have devoted as much energy as it did to fabricating evidence of immediate peril.

We hear little of Saddam's weapons, real or potential, these days. Scrambling to cloud the public memory of the principal American war aims he articulated before the conflict began, Bush has pressed, above all, to reinvent the war as one designed primarily to free the Iraqi people and build a model democracy in the Middle East. A war to destroy an adversarial regime purportedly armed with dangerous and imminently threatening weapons and allied with terrorists who slaughtered American civilians is now justified retroactively as a war that aimed to destroy Saddam Hussein's regime as such (weapons or no weapons, al-Qaeda alliances or not) and supplant it with a liberal, capitalist democracy. Such a rationale was a hard sell at home and abroad before the war began, though it found great favor with Bush's most ideologically Wilsonian, neoconservative advisors. As one of them, Paul Wolfowitz, has said, "We settled on one issue, weapons of mass destruction, because it was the one reason everyone could agree on."

But increasingly, as critic Ronald Steel observes, "Wilson has been invoked as the patron saint of the Iraq war" by Bush and his minions. On the face of it, Wilson's commitment to national self-determination and international organizations makes this seem peculiar, but as Steel says, Wilson's overriding goal was that of "constructing the world according to American principles." He sought to protect, he said, the "rights of peoples and the rights of free nations," suggesting that nations that were unfree by his lights (such as Mexico) were another matter. His internationalism was a means to "remodel the world on American lines," and useful only insofar as it proved effective to this end. Hence, one of our own New Republicans, Lawrence Kaplan, was guilty of no more than hyperbole when he declared that Bush II is "the most Wilsonian president since Wilson himself."

But I suspect that, if Bourne's ghost hovers around us, he has his eye less on Bush or on the neoconservative "right Wilsonians" than on our own "left Wilsonians." That is, it is less William Kristol, Richard Perle, and Paul Wolfowitz who would interest him than the likes of Paul Berman, Christopher Hitchens, and Michael Ignatieff, left-wing intellectuals who echoed the arguments of Dewey and other prowar progressives as they rushed to support the war in Iraq as, above all, a war for human rights and liberal democracy in the face of tyranny.

These intellectuals have had no need belatedly to move humanitarian "regime change" to the top of the list of their overt war aims since it was there from the start. They were quick to assume the posture that the European sociologist Ulrich Beck has nicely termed "military humanism." Long before Bush grabbed for a fallback rendering of the war as a human rights intervention, they were asking, as Ignatieff put it: "Who seriously believes twenty-five million Iraqis would not be better off if Saddam were overthrown?"

Since, posed in this fashion, this was at that time a question difficult to answer in the negative, one has to ask whether Bourne had anything to say that might inform the thinking of those, such as myself, who held no brief for Saddam Hussein—who are glad he is no longer with us—and yet remain as troubled by the military humanism that seeks to legitimate the war that put a noose around his neck as Bourne was by the military humanism of Dewey and

162 • RARITAN ON WAR

others of his time, however much he sympathized with their ends. What might Bourne's essays attacking the left-Wilsonian intellectuals of his day contribute to a critical assessment of the prowar stance of our own left Wilsonians?

♦ ♦ ♦

At least three things, I would say. First, one could not observe Berman, Hitchens, and Ignatieff marching to war arm in arm with Rumsfeld, Cheney, and Rove without recalling Bourne's acid comment on the strange bedfellows Dewey and other prowar intellectuals had made in 1917. "Only in a world where irony was dead," he wrote, "could an intellectual class enter war at the head of such illiberal cohorts in the avowed cause of world-liberalism and world-democracy." The contemporary left Wilsonians have been made uneasy by this alliance, but Ignatieff argues that one should not be criticized for "the company you keep" in this case, since "opposing the war doesn't make you an antiglobalist, an anti-Semite or an anti-American, any more than supporting the war makes you a Cheney conservative or an apologist for American imperialism." But Ignatieff and his left-Wilsonian comrades were not merely "keeping company" with the Bush administration, they were relying on it—as Dewey was relying on the Wilson administration—to serve their purposes. They hoped to make it their instrument.

Wilsonianism rests on the supposed coincidence of American power and international human rights: the United States is best served when people everywhere are free, and people everywhere benefit from the exercise of American power because it aims to make them free. American exceptionalism renders American hegemony, even American imperialism, benign. Right Wilsonians see the promotion of human rights as a means to ensuring the preponderance of American power; left Wilsonians see a preponderance of American power as a means to promote global human rights. Since it was the right Wilsonians who were in charge, the left Wilsonians had to hope for a coincidence of their ends with the means employed by their allies—allies whose human rights and democratization record was, shall I say, unimpressive. For much of the world, the iconic representation of the war in Iraq is not the falling statue of Saddam Hussein but a photograph of an Iraqi prisoner in American custody in the very torture chamber Saddam employed, standing hooded and half-naked on a box with electrical wire attached to his fingers. As one young Iraqi remarked, "I always knew the Americans would bring electricity back to Baghdad. I just never thought they'd be shooting it up my ass."

At their most cautious, contemporary left Wilsonians, taking account of the curious allies upon whom they were relying, argued that the spread of human rights would be the welcome, though unintended, consequence of the imperial ambitions of the right Wilsonians. John Dewey, in his more acute moments, understood that such a hope was perilously close to the "militarist's conception of war as a noble blessing in disguise," which he labeled "a stupidity." Ignatieff has subsequently admitted, "I supported an administration whose intentions I didn't trust, believing that the [unintended] consequences would repay the gamble. Now I realize that intentions do shape consequences." Here again in the face of what seem to be stunningly obvious realities of power, one sees the pull of an emotional undertow overcoming good judgment. "In a time of faith," Bourne observed, "skepticism is the most intolerable of all insults."

More often than not the unintended consequences of war are not of the happy sort that Ignatieff and other left Wilsonians envisioned. The photographs of abused prisoners from Abu Ghraib prison bring to mind another important feature of Bourne's war essays that illuminates the contemporary situation: his repeated warnings about the unpredictable and uncontrollable consequences of employing what he called the "war-technique." War, he said, "determines its own end—victory, and government crushes out automatically all forces that deflect, or threaten to deflect, energy from the path of organization to that end. All governments will act in this way, the most democratic as well as the most autocratic. . . .

164 · RARITAN ON WAR

Willing war means willing all the evils that are organically bound up with it."

War, even a just war, is likely to abridge human rights, sometimes disastrously, which is why most human rights advocates place so many strictures on the use of military force for purposes of humanitarian intervention. As Kenneth Roth, the head of Human Rights Watch, says, those advocates argue that "humanitarian intervention that occurs without the consent of the relevant government can be justified only in the face of ongoing or imminent genocide, or comparable mass slaughter or loss of life. . . . Only large-scale murder, we believe, can justify the death, destruction, and disorder that so often are inherent in war and its aftermath." In addition, Roth contends, humanitarian military action must be the last reasonable option for action; the intervention must be guided primarily by a humanitarian purpose; the intervention itself must be respectful of human rights; it must be likely that military action will do more good than harm; and such intervention is best launched by bodies with significant multilateral authority. The war in Iraq violated all of these strictures, which left Wilsonians, no less than right Wilsonians, have treated with cavalier disdain.

Chief among these strictures is the first, the requirement of a present and ongoing human rights disaster. But Saddam was not said by left Wilsonians to be murdering thousands of his people (which was not the case) but to have murdered thousands of his people (which was the case). Since the purpose of a human rights intervention is not "regime change" but an end to such disasters, the fact that no such disaster was occurring at the time of the war makes it an unjust human rights intervention. Had the United States or the United Nations intervened in 1988 when Saddam gassed the Kurds or in 1991 when he slaughtered thousands of Kurdish and Shiite opponents, a human rights intervention might well have been justified. But, of course, such an intervention did not take place, in part because the United States was complicit in these disasters. As Roth says, the absence of an ongoing human rights disaster in Iraq in the spring of 2003 is the pivotal objection to the war by most human rights advocates, for this stricture is primary, and even an intervention that meets all the other criteria is suspect. Absence of such a disaster also subverts the comparability of Iraq and Kosovo, much favored by left Wilsonians.

Finally, Bourne warns us of the dangers of putting human rights in the hands of the state, even a state as putatively different from others as the United States. His famous refrain—"War is the health of the State"—reflects his understanding of the "State" as

> essentially a concept of power, of competition; it signifies a group in its aggressive aspects. And we have the misfortune of being born not only into a country but into a State. . . . International politics is a "power politics" because it is a relation of States and that is what States infallibly and calamitously are, huge aggregations of human and industrial force that may be hurled against each other in war.

Something like this understanding of the state explains why most human rights advocates are reluctant to call on state power to protect human rights. Like war, which is its favored instrument, the state will, more likely than not, ride roughshod over human rights at home and abroad. And, as Reinhold Niebuhr noted, the state— most especially the American state—will nonetheless often cloak its quest for power in the high-minded language of a universalist ethic of human dignity.

The right Wilsonians in the Bush administration have been refreshingly candid about their imperial ambitions. Their aim is to extend American global hegemony, and they have articulated a radical doctrine of "preventive war" to that end.

Left Wilsonians have been made uneasy by this naked imperialism, but they have swallowed it. Indeed, they have in effect added an equally radical corollary of their own to the Bush Doctrine. Against the conventions of international law and the tenets

166 · RARITAN ON WAR

of just war theory, they argue that the overthrow of a tyrannical regime is grounds for unilateral humanitarian intervention by the United States. That is, they call for the United States to foster "revolution from without" in other nations wherever prudent. But as Michael Walzer argues, the long-standing and widespread understanding of what constitutes an appropriate occasion for a just humanitarian intervention is significantly less brazen:

> The occasions have to be extreme if they are to justify, perhaps even require, the use of force across an international boundary. Every violation of human rights isn't a justification. The common brutalities of authoritarian politics, the daily oppressiveness of traditional social practices—these are not occasions for intervention; they have to be dealt with locally, by the people who know the politics, who enact or resist the practices. The fact that these people can't easily or quickly reduce the incidence of brutality and oppression isn't a sufficient reason for foreigners to invade their country.

This view does not mean that, short of intervention, a nation may not institute sanctions against a tyrannical regime in the hopes of prompting an internal response, and Walzer argued for aggressive sanctions on Iraq short of war. As he said, such sanctions must themselves take account of humanitarian concerns, and seek to avoid measures such as some of those trade restrictions adopted against Iraq before the war that punished innocent Iraqis without any effect on Saddam and his henchmen. I suspect that, given his argument for "armed neutrality" in World War I, Bourne might have found this position appealing, and would, at least, have supported the call for more "coercive inspections" than those undertaken by the United Nations in Iraq, a policy advocated by the Carnegie Endowment before the war.

But such an aggressive human rights policy falls far short of revolution from without. The military humanism of the left Wilsonians, no less than the ambitious imperialism of the right Wilsonians, makes the state of the United States the arbiter of the domestic politics of the rest of the world—the judge, jury, and executioner of all regimes that fail to meet its liberal-democratic standards, standards it claims are universal. As David Rieff points out, the "central idea of committing the United States to foster democratic change throughout the world, at the point of a gun if there is no other alternative, unites the liberal internationalist position and the neoconservative position in ways that bemuse conservatives and tend to push liberal interventionists into paroxysms of denial." But whatever their denials, theirs is "a program for endless wars of altruism."

Hence, Bourne might say, left Wilsonians were betrayed in Iraq less by a shortsighted alliance with right Wilsonians than by the hubris they shared with them. Their stance, like that of the neoconservatives, is American exceptionalism with a (literal) vengeance. Both assume an America capable of surmounting the risks of military humanism and obliged to do so. As such, both portend an imperial American state steadfastly poised in the missionary position.

◆　◆　◆

The Wilsonian war in Iraq has over the course of more than four years become itself a humanitarian disaster, and the country has descended into the civil war that some predicted before the invasion. Along with thousands of American soldiers, tens of thousands of Iraqi civilians have died, and Ignatieff's confident assertion that they are better off in the wake of an American-led revolution from without no longer passes unchallenged, at least by many Iraqis.

What now do we do in Iraq? we might ask the ghost of Randolph Bourne. This is not a question that affords any clear or easy answers. The pragmatism that Bourne practiced and Dewey betrayed during World War I does not promise any moral algorithms for awful situations such as this. In these circumstances, it seems certain that we must "butcher the ideal," as William James said. We must, that

168 • RARITAN ON WAR

is, weigh the imponderable consequences of sooner or later ending the American occupation, choosing with little confidence among a set of unhappy alternatives that will in every instance do little to deter years more of death and destruction in Iraq. As Bourne remarked of his war, "The final solution will neither be short nor soon. There are too many old crimes unpunished, too many spoliations unrecompensed, to make this struggle anything but the prelude to a long series of laborious adjustments." It is not a question of avoiding a bloodbath in Iraq, since a bloodbath is well underway. It is probably a matter of avoiding one bloodbath in favor of another.

I suspect Bourne might suggest that this is not a choice for the United States alone to make, unless we are willing to own up frankly to imperial ambitions. It is time to take seriously the Wilsonian value our Wilsonians tend to underplay—self-determination—and admit that the United States may well have contributed to a situation in Iraq in which it can no longer be of much assistance in Iraqi self-determination. One reason that the Bush administration is reluctant to admit that Iraq is in the grip of a civil war (as well as witness to a successful Kurdish secession movement) is that, as Walzer says, "once a community is effectively divided, foreign powers can hardly serve the cause of self-determination by acting militarily within its borders." If policymakers do indeed believe that Iraqi self-determination is the principal American objective for post-Saddam Iraq, as Bush avows, then they should bring the troops home and allow the Iraqis their own (now inevitably bloody) revolution from within. Even if, as the case may be, it means the end of Iraq.

The reason that self-determination is the Wilsonian value that Wilsonians have usually honored only in the breach is that they come to the project with a single self in mind, their own. As Dean Acheson nicely put it, "We are willing to help people who believe the way we do to continue to live the way they want to live." The Iraqi nation that will emerge from the ruins, if it is indeed one nation, is likely to be a nasty affair, and not one ruled by people who believe the way we do. They should be allowed to go their own way, so long as they pose no genuine and imminent threat to American security. And so long as they do not assume the posture of Arab (or Kurdish) Hutus and Tutsis. If that happens, then we must hope that the cause of justifiable humanitarian intervention has not been irreparably damaged by this war.

Randolph Bourne did think that a disastrous war might be of some use, "if it shakes us out of our fatuous complacency of shibboleths and creeds, and makes us long for a clear and radiant civilization as a lover desires his bride." He would, he said, "have nothing to do with those who would say that such a lesson would justify the war," yet he allowed that "such reflections may serve to lighten a little these hours of disillusionment and permit us to meet with faith and hope whatever darker hours are yet to come." So might we again pray.

Summer 2007

The Man Who Knew Too Much
LYLE JEREMY RUBIN

SUPPOSE A GRAVE-LOOKING MAN, after approaching you on the sidewalk, announced that the government had contingency plans to annihilate the bulk of humanity and most large nonhuman species to boot. Odds are you would offer a nervous grin or grimace and pick up your pace. Imagine this same man kept track and informed you he had once served in the highest reaches of the national-security bureaucracy as a nuclear-war expert when such plans were being hatched, and not much has changed since then. At this point you might search for a convenient storefront or café to make your prompt escape. But what if your unwelcome inter-locutor then grabbed you by your cuff and warned of "a catastro-phe waiting to happen!" What then?

It is an uncomfortable hypothetical, although not as uncomfort-able as the fact that someone like this man does exist, and every-thing he has to say is credible. His name is Daniel Ellsberg. In the introduction to *The Doomsday Machine: Confessions of a Nuclear War Planner*, the historic whistleblower of Pentagon Papers fame cuts to the chase: "The hidden reality I aim to expose is that for over fifty years, all-out thermonuclear war—an irreversible, unprecedented, and almost unimaginable calamity for civilization and most life on earth—has been, like the disasters of Chernobyl, Katrina, the Gulf oil spill, Fukushima Daiichi, and before these, World War I, *a catastrophe waiting to happen*, on a scale infinitely greater than any of these. And this is still true today." The argument is straightforward, and it suggests a kind of collective madness that dwarfs the eccentricities of any pavement malcontent. Ever since the Soviets acquired the bomb in 1949, game theorists on each end of the Cold War divide, along with eventual bomb-wielding newcomers in the United Kingdom, France, China, Israel, India,

Pakistan, and North Korea, have been preparing for one another's mutual destruction. Except they've told themselves it was just the other guy who would end up destroyed. Ellsberg divulges some of Washington's casualty estimates, and they are not for the fainthearted. During the height of the standoff in Berlin in August of 1961, for example, the Joint Chiefs of Staff were poised to launch a preemptive first-strike attack against Russia and China that anticipated 325 million deaths within six months. This didn't cover the expected one hundred million lives lost in Europe, as well as another one hundred million across Russia and China's periphery. Thankfully, as one officer at the Strategic Air Command reassured Ellsberg at the time, "less than ten million" lives in the United States risked being claimed in retaliation.

But these numbers told only the half of it. As Ellsberg and others suspected, resulting firestorms were likely to prove fatal for anyone present within two to five times the blast radius. This meant, at minimum, a billion people were at risk, a third of Earth's population in 1961. And as climate scientists in 1983 concluded, the remaining two billion were also likely to expire from the firestorm's gargantuan billows of smoke, which would envelop the stratosphere like a mortal quilt, occluding sunlight for a decade and devastating life-sustaining crops. Such a nuclear winter is even more plausible today, now that each contemporary hydrogen bomb requires a 1940s-vintage A-bomb merely as its detonator. The notorious iconography of Hiroshima or Nagasaki only accounts, in Ellsberg's words, for "what happens to humans and buildings when they are hit by what is now just the detonating cap for a modern nuclear weapon."

Lest you believe the prospect for thermonuclear war is a thing of the past, consider this: the *Bulletin of the Atomic Scientists* has the Doomsday Clock at one hundred seconds to midnight, the closest it's ever been to apocalypse since concerned veterans of the Manhattan Project inaugurated the measurement in 1947. This calculation derives both from increasingly reckless leadership around the globe and certain provocations in particular. The Trump administration

172 • RARITAN ON WAR

has withdrawn from the Intermediate-Range Nuclear Forces Treaty, a response to supposed noncompliance on the part of Putin's government. This has opened the floodgates for the development and expansion of riskier weapons that can reach their destination within ten minutes, foreclosing the possibility of any fair warning or cool-headed deliberation. The withdrawal has also encouraged a new nuclear arms race, one that involves not only the United States and Russia, but China too. Such foolhardiness has been accompanied by Trump's nixing of the Joint Comprehensive Plan of Action with Iran and by North Korea's continuing brinkmanship. The cessation of the New Strategic Arms Reduction Treaty (New START) next year looms on the horizon. Then there are accelerated tensions between India and Pakistan, continued bedlam in Syria—a conflict embroiling more than half of the world's nuclear powers—and U.S. investment in low-yield ballistic warheads. Embrace of the latter development is based on the premise that low-level nukes, launched by submarine, can be deployed without triggering full-scale nuclear Armageddon. But since radar has a high probability of mistaking these missiles for their larger counterparts, all this buildup does is increase the likelihood of a final judgment.

When Ellsberg was still working for Uncle Sam, he conducted numerous interviews with uniformed service members tasked with one day executing a nuclear strike. What he discovered was terrifying. Pilots admitted that under a series of high-stakes circumstances, including the loss of communication with higher-ups, they would abandon protocol and launch their warheads. Communications then, as now, were characteristically spotty, and false alarms concerning enemy nuclear attacks were not uncommon. The same went for these pilots' supervisors, one of whom boasted about being willing to violate failsafe directives designed to preclude accidental or unnecessary nuclear war. Ellsberg, at the time of his investigation in 1959 and 1960, found myriad ways that bad actors within and without the military could initiate an unlawful nuclear order, in large part because authorization had been so widely devolved and subdelegated. And he makes a strong case that military leadership and culture as a whole leaned toward "Go" in cases of ambiguity or uncertainty, while leaning against civilian veto power. If this sounds too much like the script from *Dr. Strangelove*, that's because the book on which that film was based, *Red Alert*, was written by a former Royal Air Force Bomber Command flight officer who was appalled by the same institutional loopholes and deranged ethos. Ellsberg fears much of that ethos is still operative, and hints of its persistence have been recorded at watchdog venues like the Nuclear Information Project at the Federation of American Scientists.

Although the military's successes at sealing off nuclear prerogatives from civilian control are troubling, it is not as if civilian command has been more enlightened. For decades the American political class in both parties agreed to keep nuclear-armed warships ashore in Japanese ports without the Japanese government's official approval, thus putting the country at risk of another, albeit more calamitous, Hiroshima or Nagasaki in the case of an accident or any scenario in which an enemy of the United States was set on activating a first strike. The policy toward Japan follows a long pattern of disregard for the survival of non-Americans, even America's most trusted allies. It was standard operating procedure throughout the Cold War for all of China to be blasted into oblivion if the United States ever found itself in armed conflict with a Russian brigade or division. Eisenhower supported this because he worried that conventional armed conflict with the Soviet Union would lead to excessive inflation, depression, and bankruptcy, and figured any attempt at a quick-win nuclear closure would entail China taking the side of Russia. What's more, since planners didn't acknowledge Russian brigades and divisions were often undermanned, comprising fewer battalions than assumed, the threshold for setting off a nuclear exchange and wiping out humanity was lower than it should have been.

These revelations may make up the most shocking sections of Ellsberg's memoir, but it is at its most affecting in its history of

174 • RARITAN ON WAR

modern assault on civilians. From General Sherman's burning of Atlanta and terrorist march to the sea to the Luftwaffe's bombing of Guernica during the Spanish Civil War to Japan's massacre in Nanjing to the British and American firebombing of Dresden and Tokyo . . . the basic outlines themselves do nothing but haunt. But it is in the details that the true horror resides. General Curtis LeMay's doctrine of "strategic bombing"—the mass targeting of noncombatants, specifically industrial workers, designed to decimate enemy logistics and morale—came straight from Mussolini's air commissioner, Giulio Douhet. As late as 1943, plenty of U.S. air officers still considered Britain's indiscriminate air raids of German cities barbaric, echoing President Roosevelt's words about the savagery of targeting urban areas four years before. But by 1945, General George Marshall was itching, by his own admission, to "set the paper cities of Japan on fire." This was the same time LeMay was asking his weather officer for Tokyo how strong the wind had to be "so that people can't get away from the flames." He followed up, "Will the wind be strong enough for that?"

LeMay continued to lead from the highest reaches of the U.S. government under presidents Truman, Eisenhower, Kennedy, and Johnson, all of whom had faith that such a man would carry out his responsibilities with utmost excellence as commander of the Strategic Air Command and then chief of staff of the U.S. Air Force. But LeMay's extraordinary tenure as America's top-dog executioner was a symptom of a larger problem, the same problem that has propelled American complicity in the destruction of places like Korea, Vietnam, Laos, Iraq, and Libya; genocide in places like Indonesia, East Timor, Cambodia, and Yemen; oppression in places like Iran, Guatemala, Congo, Chile, Egypt, and Saudi Arabia; and occupations in places like Palestine and Afghanistan. It is the problem of the gradual normalization of extreme systematic violence, a normalization cheered on by ostensible scientific improvements. Humans have been normalizing such violence for well over a century now, at least since mass killing and policing machines first came on the scene. Americans, however, seem to have forged a proud identity around it. If the rest of the international community isn't trying hard enough to pull back from the brink, U.S. officials behave as if there is no brink, or as if, in the words of Pangloss, we are still living in the best of all possible worlds. The refusal of the United States and NATO to adopt a no-first-use policy regarding their nuclear arsenal, combined with their recent acceleration of the nuclear arms race, speaks to a deeper moral rot that has been decades in the making, and a rot that, if left untreated, jeopardizes everyone and everything.

Such a death drive may not have reached its natural end quite yet, but it hasn't lain dormant either. The problem is not only that the bellicosity behind America's unhinged nuclear policies is the same bellicosity informing so much of the national-security state's interventions and collusions abroad. It is that the two are connected in more material ways. Henry Kissinger, in his capacity as national security advisor and secretary of state under Nixon, threatened North Vietnam with a nuclear strike twelve times as a means of gaining the upper hand in various deadlocks. Ellsberg asserts that such a threat has been employed or discussed with the Joint Chiefs of Staff no less than twenty-five times, and he documents all twenty-five cases in *Doomsday Machine*, in situations ranging from the Berlin crisis to the Cuban missile crisis to the 1973 Arab-Israeli War, the last of which effectively warded off Soviet assistance to beleaguered Egyptian troops. This gun-to-the-head tactic, in Ellsberg's reckoning, has probably been used in numerous other classified instances, and it has always played a central role in maintaining the U.S.-led global order.

Ellsberg has spent half a century exposing and opposing the underbelly of that order, and since the initial glow of the Pentagon Papers, political and media elites seem to have become progressively uninterested in what he has to say. He might not be demonized like Edward Snowden or Julian Assange, or held in contempt like Chelsea Manning, but it's fair to say his jeremiads through the years have often been politely ignored, whether they've related to

176 • RARITAN ON WAR

the harrowing costs of America's wars or its surveillance state. Such is the fate of those who dare to challenge rather than reinforce status-quo power relations. For those who go the route of reinforcement, or whose whistleblowing takes that form whether they intend it or not, inordinate attention or plaudits are inevitable. This helps explain the lavish praise heaped on the CIA employee responsible for disclosing Trump's notorious phone call with Ukrainian president Volodymyr Zelensky, or the corroborating witness testimony of Lieutenant Colonel Alexander Vindman. The very fact their labors heralded impeachment was enough to make them heroes in the eyes of most Democrats. But it was also how their disclosures came to launder otherwise questionable American meddling alongside Russia's borders, or the supposed nobility of the U.S. intelligence agencies and broader national-defense leviathan, that made their public service especially valuable.

To regret the absence of any serious mention of subjects like no first use, New START, low-yield nuclear weapons, or the Comprehensive Nuclear Test Ban Treaty in the mainstream discourse, including the presidential debates of late, constitutes a reasonable and necessary response. Such an absence is mad. To find the relevant discourse reduced to the sole hazards of darker-skinned, "third world" governments in the Global South, namely Iran and North Korea, acquiring or utilizing nuclear capabilities is equally maddening. So are attempts to portray those who have sought de-escalation between the world's two great nuclear powers as somehow anti-American, as the *New York Times* attempted not long ago with regard to Bernie Sanders's participation in a sister-cities program with the Soviet Union in the eighties. But the most maddening fact of all is the popular failure to see the nuclear lunacy fleshed out by Ellsberg within a wider living history of domination and bloodshed. Or even to see those lives and societies already dying or barely surviving all around us, all amid the so-called American peace.

Summer 2020

The Animals of the Budapest Zoo, 1944–1945
TAMAS DOBOZY

IT WAS SÁNDOR who finally posed the question in November of 1944, when it was clear the Red Army would take Budapest from the Arrow Cross and the Nazis. "If there's a siege, how are we going to protect the animals?" he asked, looking from one face to the next, totally baffled by the fact that everyone seemed far more interested in how they were going to protect themselves. "We're going to have to work double hard," replied Oszkár Teleki, director of the zoo, though Teleki would be the first to run off that December when the Russian tanks entered the squares and boulevards, telling his secretary he was going to meet with the Red Army and insist that they respect the animals, and then asking her to pack all of the zoo's money into a bag, just in case.

Sándor and József were the last to see Teleki leave, intercepting him near the exit and asking whether he had plans in place for the aquarium, where even now the attendants were working around the clock to keep the water from freezing by stirring it with paddles. Both men were suspicious because Teleki was wearing an overcoat belted at the waist and an elegant hat, and was carrying an ivory-handled umbrella in one hand and a suitcase bulging with money in the other, banknotes fluttering from every crack. Also, Teleki wasn't taking the eastern exit out of the zoo, as he normally did when going home, but the western one, in the direction of Buda, of Germany, and away from the advancing Soviets.

"We should feed you to the lion," said Sándor, to which Teleki responded by fingering his collar and looking nervous and telling them he'd be back "really quite soon." "You're not going anywhere," said József, and he grabbed hold of Teleki as he was turning from

178 • RARITAN ON WAR

them, jerking him so hard the old man's knees gave out and József had to hold him up above the muddy cobblestones.

József was about to do something else to him then—hit him, or pull the suitcase from his grip—but when he saw Teleki's face—the bared teeth, the eyes darting back and forth, the desperation to escape—looking just like the animals did whenever there was an air raid, an explosion of shells, the rattle of gunfire, flames shooting over the palisades, he let him go, knowing that the money would soon have as little currency as a fascist armband. But if he'd looked a little closer he might have caught something else in Teleki's face as well, the city's future in its wrinkles and lines, a vision of what the next hundred days would be like, when Budapest's populace would be driven to looting and stealing and scavenging and murder, a city in which only on the faces of the dead—and there would be many of those, down by the banks of the Danube where the Arrow Cross executed the Jewish men, women, and children after marching them naked through the snow from the ghetto; or Széll Kálmán Square after the failure of Hungarian and German soldiers to break through the Soviet encirclement, bodies piled in doorways and cellar stairs and in other piles of bodies in an attempt to shield themselves from the rockets and snipers and tanks the Red Army had stationed along the routes they knew the fleeing soldiers would take—only on those faces could you see what Sándor whispered about to József at night, the thing he was more and more obsessed with as the siege dragged on, the metamorphosis at work all around them. And in the early days, when József was still alert, still sane enough to ask him what the hell he was talking about, Sándor muttered about human beings turning into "flowers and animals," and held up Ovid, or some other book he'd stolen from the abandoned library in Teleki's office, and whistled quietly, reading quietly, until József fell back asleep.

It got so bad that József would need that whistling to sleep, and when it stopped, late at night, and József snapped awake, more often than not he found that Sándor wasn't there, gone into the night or disappeared, expending himself as if to prove that becoming nothing could be a transformation too. He was always back by morning, though, with his dirty nails and oily face and tattered clothes and the look of someone who'd lost himself along the way.

◆ ◆ ◆

But before all that, December turned into January. Unlike many of the other attendants, Sándor and József did not have families, and so they saw no reason to go home from the zoo and risk dying in the streets, or being bombed out of their tiny apartments, or starving to death in the cellars that had been converted into bomb shelters. And when the zebras were found slaughtered in their pens, large strips of meat carved hastily from their shoulders and flanks and bellies no doubt by starving citizens, the two men fed what was left to the lion and moved into the vacated stalls, and Sándor ranted about how the zebras should still be alive and how it was the looters who should have been fed to the lion.

When Márti, another of the attendants, was shot in late January as she was trying to tear up a bit of grass for the giraffe in the nearby Városliget and somehow managed to stumble back to the zoo, she described in a sleepy voice what she had seen out there in the city. Sándor tried to get her to be quiet, to rest, pulling the blanket to her chin as she spoke of the shapes of flame as a child might speak of clouds, seeing in them animals dead or dying, their souls somehow escaping the bodies trapped in the zoo, transmigrated into fire, taking revenge on the city. She said it was burning, all of it—the Western Station, the mansions along Andrássy Boulevard, the trees in the park like used matchsticks. She'd seen a street where blue flame was dancing through every pothole and crack, playing round the rim of craters, the gas mains ruptured underneath, continuing to bleed. "It was like a celebration," said Márti, before closing her eyes and falling into a sleep neither József nor Sándor tried waking her from.

180 • RARITAN ON WAR

The night after she died, they climbed the roof of the palm garden, which gave them a view beyond the palisades toward where the fighting was going on, now far to the west, mortars and tanks and bullets pounding the lower battlements of Buda castle, flashes of white light whenever the smoke cleared. The sky held odd things—crates tied to parachutes falling onto the ice over the Danube; gliders crashing at night, guided by spotlights into trees and buildings; ash rising like a million flies.

Sándor was trying to keep reading during those days, scrambling up a ladder to Teleki's library after the air raid destroyed the staircase, as if the books were more than a distraction, as if they were necessary to hurry his mind along, as if it were possible to stop thinking by thinking too much, by exploding thought, at a time when having a mind was, more often than not, a handicap. Of the two of them he'd always been the one given to dreams, and as they sat on the roof of the palm garden that night, Sándor spoke to József of what he'd discovered in Teleki's office: an entire library, books ancient and modern, devoted to the subject of animals. "I had no idea Teleki was such an intellectual," growled Sándor above the crackling of guns, and then he began to speak of how characters in myths and stories and fairy tales turned into horses and flowers and hounds and back again, or into other people entirely, crossing limits as if they didn't exist, becoming something else. "But now, I mean *now*," he waved his arms around as if he could encompass the last five centuries, "now we don't transform. We're *individuals* now. *Selves*. Fixed in place."

"Well," said József, his head turning over Sándor's ideas. "What difference does it make? They died in wars just like us."

"Maybe that's how they explained death," said Sándor, his face glazed with the light of nearby fires. "Becoming something else." He gazed down through the glass roof of the palm house. "Anyhow, we're not dead yet," he purred, flexing his fingers, József thought, as if they could become claws.

"But did they stay themselves, I mean, when they became something else?"

"That's just it. There was no self to begin with. Just an endless transformation, a constant becoming."

"So then a lion was worth the same as a human being."

"Well, I don't know about 'worth,'" said Sándor, smiling at József. "But there wasn't the same way of telling the differ . . ."

But before Sándor could take the idea any further, he was already crashing through the roof of the palm garden as the shell exploded, disappearing into the fire and shock waves and rain of glass, while József was able to scramble down before the next mortar fell whistling into the hole the last one had made, scrambling down, and then through the cracked doors of the glass building, shards raining all around, the alligators and hippos of the central exhibit too shocked to snap or charge at him, lifting Sándor's body from where it lay face down in a pool of water, and smiling despite himself when his friend began spluttering, bruises spreading across his face. Two days later, the alligators died, frozen stiff in their ice-encrusted jungle, though the hippos lived on, drawn to the very back of the tank, where the artesian well kept pumping out its thermal waters, the fat on their stomachs and backs thinning away as it fed them, all three growing skinnier and skinnier in the steam.

◆　◆　◆

Later, when Lieutenant General Zamertsev questioned József about the lion, trying to get him to reveal where it was hiding, József resisted by speaking instead about the alligators and hippos, about the destruction of the palm garden as the moment where Sándor and he realized they would have to "liberate" as many of the animals as they could. Zamertsev looked at him, and then turned to the Hungarian interpreter and whispered something, and then the interpreter said to József, "You actually thought it was a good idea to let the lions and panthers and cougars and wolves roam free?"

182 • RARITAN ON WAR

József knew that Zamertsev didn't believe him, that he was not accusing him of excessive sentimentality so much as lying, or maybe outright craziness, as if between the destruction of the siege and Sándor's ranting, József's brain had also become unhinged. And Zamertsev was right in a sense, because it wasn't what happened to the alligators that made Sándor and him wander around the zoo unlocking cages, but rather the arrival of the Soviet soldiers, Zamertsev's men, high atop their horses, demanding that the zoo-keepers first release a wolf, and then a leopard, and then a tiger, all so the soldiers could hunt these half-starved creatures that could barely walk, never mind run, chasing the animals down with fresh horses and military ordnance, drunk and laughing and twice crazy with what the war had both taken from and permitted them.

The attendants were into the champagne that night, having discovered a crate of the expensive stuff in one of the locked trunks Teleki left in his office, along with several sealed tins of caviar and a box of excellent cigars, Sándor handing out bottles and tins and matches to József and Gergő and Zsuzsi, all of them so hungry and tired of thinking about what might happen to them the following week, or tomorrow, or the next minute that they popped the corks as fast as possible and began drinking, trying to wash from themselves the cold and fear and the dead animals all around, as if by concentrating they could keep only to the taste of what was on their tongues, and think of nothing else.

It was of course Sándor's idea, the action he decided on after he'd drained his second bottle of Törley, leaving off the caviar, looking at everyone's grubby knuckles, their wincing with the sound of another explosion or rattle of gunfire or the slow fall of flares (falling so crookedly they seemed to be welding fractures in the sky). And so it was neither love nor logic that led them around the zoo that night but drunkenness, jingling keys pulled from Teleki's walls, moving past the carcasses in the monkey house, many of them frozen to the bars they'd been gripping when their heat gave out and they laid their heads onto their shoulders welcoming the last warmth of sleep; or in the tropical aviary, the brightly colored feathers gone dull on the curled forms, their heads dusted with frost and tangled in the netting overhead, as close as they would ever again come to the sun; or in the aquarium, where someone now gone, perhaps Márti, had broken through the glass of the tanks and tried to chip some of the fish out of the ice, whether in some pathetic attempt to thaw them back to life or to eat them no one could guess. In the end, it was less an organized act than a celebration, less motivated by reason or a goal than a delight in the moment when the cage swung open and something else bounded or crawled or slithered or flew out, the four of them downing champagne and running around, eagerly seeking the next thrill of release, opening after opening, an orgy of smashing those locks they'd worried over for years. And when it was over, when there wasn't a single cage left to open, an animal left to free, then Gergö and Zsuzsi freed themselves, waltzing out the front gate straight into a warning shout, a halting laugh, a hail of machine-gun fire.

◆ ◆ ◆

Which brought József and Sándor back to themselves in a hurry. "I'll bet it did," said Zamertsev, leaning over the table and staring at József, the shoulders and chest of his uniform covered with red stars and hammers and sickles and decorative ribbons. "And I guess that's when you got the idea of feeding my soldiers to the lion."

"It was your soldiers' horses we wanted," mumbled József, still so amazed by the last sound Sándor had made—he could imagine him tossing his head and baring his teeth and roaring so loudly it could be heard above the guns—that József might have been speaking to anybody, treating Zamertsev as though he was an acquaintance he'd met in a restaurant or café rather than someone who at any moment could have sent him out to be shot. "A lion can live a lot longer on a horse than a man, you know."

But the truth is he wasn't sure, for Sándor had frequently looked down upon the Russian soldiers (both from the roof of the palm

184 · RARITAN ON WAR

garden, and later from the palisades) and licked his dry lips and recalled the Siege of Leningrad, wondering if people in Budapest would end up eating human flesh, as they were rumored to have done there. At the time, József had not connected Sándor's actions with appetite, but with a hatred of the Soviets, because with all the dead German and Arrow Cross soldiers, not to mention civilians lying in the streets, perfectly preserved by a winter so cold even the Danube had frozen over, there was no need to hunt the living. And Sándor had made strange references to the Soviets and the Red Army as the two men wandered around the zoo in the waning days of the siege, when most of the fires in Pest had gone out and the Russians were mopping up what was left of the enemy by marching Hungarian men and women through the streets and forcing them to call out, "Don't shoot, don't shoot, we're Hungarians, give yourselves up"; though to the west the fighting was still thick, relentless, out there across the Danube, on the Buda side of the city, where the Nazis and Arrow Cross were holed up on Castle Hill, surrounded, running out of ammunition and food, dreaming of a breakout.

Of the animals they'd released, a few vultures and eagles remained, circling above the zoo and drifting lazily down to feed on the plentiful carrion in the streets. When they returned to their nests, Sándor would wonder what was more poisonous in their bellies, the flesh of communists or fascists. He would say things like that. And when they held discussions, long into the night, and József said the fascists were wrong to speak of their beliefs, the society they envisaged, as natural, for no animal was ever interested in war for glory, or compiling lists of atrocities, or mastering the world, or getting rid, en masse, of another species, and that more often than not what animals did was tend only to their immediate needs, and in doing so created a kind of harmony . . . "Harmony?" laughed Sándor. "You sound like a communist!" And he spoke of how a male grizzly will kill the cubs belonging to another male so that the female will mate with him; how he'd once heard about a weasel that came into a yard and killed twenty-five chickens, biting them through the neck, without taking a single one of the corpses to eat; how certain gulls will steal eggs from others, sit on them until they hatch, and then feed the chicks to their own young; how a cat will play with whatever it catches, torturing it slowly to death, all out of amusement. "Does that sound like *harmony* to you?" he asked József.

Zamertsev looked a moment at József, who sat there trembling in the creaking chair in the headquarters the Red Army had put up in one of the half-obliterated mansions along Andrássy Boulevard, still dressed in the ragged attendant's uniform, unwashed these hundred days, his hair matted and filthy, so shriveled by hunger Zamertsev thought he could see the man's spine poking through the skin of a belly fallen in on its emptiness. And then Zamertsev came around the desk and grabbed József's chin roughly in one hand and said, "I'm not interested in what you think I want to hear. Politics . . ." He looked at the interpreter, who raised his eyebrows. "I want to protect my . . . the people's army . . . which means telling me about Sándor, what he did, what I'm dealing with . . ."

Protect the people's army. József wanted to laugh. If your soldiers had been kept in check, if they hadn't come in wanting a safari all their own, we wouldn't have had to free the animals in the first place. And after they freed the animals, Sándor seemed intent on prowling around the place as if he were one of them, even though József warned him to stay inside, because there wasn't a day when one of the carnivores that was still alive didn't come upon another, the polar bear devouring the wolves, the wolves taking apart the panther, the lion emerging at night. But that's how it was then: József working hard to conserve himself, to survive, while Sándor had given up on everything—first sleep, then food, then safety— divesting himself of every resource.

Somehow Sándor had gotten word to the Russians that the lion was living in the tunnels of the subway, and when the other predators were gone—having finally eaten one another, or been shot, or wandered off—then the lion took to eating stray horses, and

186 • RARITAN ON WAR

Sándor would point out its victims to József when they went out to gather snow for drinking water, Sándor hobbling along, weakened enough by then to need the help of one of Teleki's canes, though he still had enough presence of mind to show József how it was teeth, not ordnance, that had made the gaping holes along the flanks and backs and bellies of the horses. "The lion must be weakened," said Sándor, clutching himself, "otherwise, it would have dragged the carcass away to where it lives, and eaten the whole thing."

"Or maybe it's too full to bother," said József, envious of its teeth.

At night, József would awaken and not even turn toward Sándor's pallet, because he knew he wasn't there. Night after night he'd awaken and Sándor would be out. Sleepwalking is what József thought at first, but when he asked about it, Sándor would laugh and say he'd been out "getting horses." There wasn't a lot to what Sándor said anymore, though truth to tell József himself was having trouble coming up with anything to say, and with saying it, when he did, in a meaningful way.

"My soldiers tell me Sándor was meeting with them," said Zamertsev. "That he was arranging lion hunts in the subway tunnels."

"You could fit a herd of horses into there," nodded József. "But it was very dark. And the soldiers were always drunk. And there were bullets flying all over the place."

"It was one way to feed the lion," said Zamertsev. "And you knew about it. Perhaps even helped him?"

No, József shook his head, and then a second later, he nodded yes, and then stopped, not knowing who or what he'd helped, deciding that it certainly wasn't Sándor. Zamertsev was wrong to think that Sándor was feeding the lion, for that's what József had thought at first as well, as if the lion and Sándor were two separate things. But it was better that Zamertsev think this than what József knew to be the truth, the transformation he'd witnessed the day he'd carried Sándor to the subway entrance, one of the few that weren't bombed out or buried in rubble or so marked by the lion's presence that even humans could sense the danger there. He'd pressed his body against the door—it was an old service entrance used by the engineers and subway personnel, wide enough to fit a small car, covered with corrugated metal—envisioning that awful metamorphosis.

◆　◆　◆

But as it turned out Zamertsev wasn't like the other soldiers, so easily led into the same trap. He sent for one of his men and told him to get a map of the old Franz Joseph Underground Line, staring silently at József until the blueprints were delivered, at which point he spread them across the desk and began tracing the possible routes into and out of the subway, ignoring entirely the service entrance József had told him about. It was as if he knew, József thought, as if he'd discerned the bits of the story József had left out, and was even now being guided over the map by what József hadn't told him of that last night, when Sándor had crawled over and whispered to him of the effort of getting horses for the lion, of how weak he'd become, though what József really heard in his voice was a hunger so great it would have swallowed him then and there if Sándor had had the strength, if he felt he could have overpowered his friend. "I can't do it alone," Sándor mumbled. "I can't walk." And when József asked if their friendship no longer meant anything to him, Sándor rubbed the place in his skull where his cheeks had been and said something about "word getting around," and the soldiers "staying away," and then paused and smiled that terrible smile, lipless, all teeth. "It's because I'm your friend that I'm asking you to do this. There is no greater thing a friend could do," he said, laughing without a trace of happiness.

　　József had looked at him then, turning from where he'd been facing the wall, hugging himself as if in consolation for the emptiness of his stomach, for the delirium of this siege without end, the constant fear, the boredom, waiting on the clock, the slow erasure of affection, of the list of things he would not do. "The city is

188 • RARITAN ON WAR

destroyed," he said, not wanting to do as Sándor asked, not wanting even to address it, for he thought he'd caught another implication in his voice now, one even worse than what his words had first suggested. "There are people dead and starving," he continued, "the Soviets are looting, hunting, raping, and you're worried about a lion. *Fuck the lion*," said József, "fuck everything," and he turned over on his pallet, lifting the layers of plastic sacks and tarpaulin they used for blankets. But Sándor nudged him again, and when József let out an exasperated moan and turned, he saw that his friend was already half transformed, the hair wild around his head and neck, his fingernails much longer than József's, and dirtier too, packed underneath with the hide and flesh of horses and men and what else, reduced from malnourishment and injury and trauma to crawling around on all fours. "I need you," growled Sándor, though he had lost so much by then that it came out like a cough, the chords in his throat too slack, or worn, for much noise, and it cost him to raise his voice above a whimper.

Need me, wondered József, rising from the sheets and drawing Sándor's head to his chest. You don't know what you need, he thought, as if there were two pulses beating in counter-rhythm within Sándor, two desires moving him in opposite directions. He held him like that for a while, feeling his friend's eyelids blinking regularly against his skin, thinking of how Sándor had run out of the zoo after Gergö and Zsuzsi, trying to gather up their limp forms, of how often they'd found him squatting in the cage of this or that dead animal, as if he believed that by lifting a wing or an arm or a leg he might reanimate them, or, as József had once observed, actually putting on the animal like a suit of clothes, becoming it and leaving his humanity behind. And all the while Sándor had been going in the opposite direction, trying to keep in mind who he was, who he'd been, what he cared about.

"Listen, Sándor," he murmured, frightened by what was taking place in his friend's body, the spasms that passed through it as he held him. "You have to pull yourself together," he said, "the siege won't last forever." But Sándor was already past the idea of waiting, József knew that, past thinking about what had happened and what was to come. What he really wanted, what he needed, had nothing to do with József at all, for József was already disappearing for Sándor, disintegrating into the state of war, falling apart with the capital and the zoo, with the death of all the animals—and all he needed to complete it was this one last act, this final favor. But it wasn't like that for József, not yet, for Sándor was still keeping him intact, as if the strength of their friendship, the history they shared, whatever it was in his character that Sándor loved, could recall József to himself. He looked at Sándor and saw what the war had done to friendship after it had finished with everything else—with sympathy, with intelligence, with self-awareness, with loyalty and affection and love—all those impediments to survival, all those things that got in the way of forgetting who you were. And it was for this that József envied Sándor, for Sándor had forgotten him just as he'd forgotten that the soldiers he'd fed to the lion were men, that the bodies the birds fed on were those of women and children, that there was even such a thing as his own life, or anyone else's, and that it might be worth preserving.

When he finally rose up with Sándor that night, carrying him in his arms like a child, József wasn't sure if he could do what Sándor wanted him to do, because he was still clinging to his friend's memory, unwilling to let him go, as he would weeks later, even more so, after the conversation with Zamertsev, after the Soviet hunting party had gone out—sober this time, no horses—carrying flashlights and headlamps, determined to do it right. He had set out that night in exactly the same way, out the door, moving along, bent with Sándor's weight under arc lights and stuttering streetlamps, dodging patrols that weren't really patrols but an extension of the three days of free looting the commanders had granted their troops.

By then he knew what Sándor needed as much as Sándor did—this is what József would not tell Zamertsev—and when they arrived at the subway entrance and swung open the door and looked inside,

190 • RARITAN ON WAR

József hesitated. And when Sándor, resting his head against his chest, told him just to put him down on the threshold, József laughed and said it was fine, they could go in together, it didn't matter. "No," said Sándor, jerking limply in József's arms. "You've been better with your grief," he said, "better able to use it—to help make yourself stronger." And with this, József finally understood what Sándor wanted, and why, and József would remember it as the moment when he finally gave in to the siege, to its terrible logic, to what Sándor hoped to become, what he needed József—his last friend in the world—to witness. He said goodbye too, before putting Sándor down there, and closing the door on him. Then there was only the weakness, from carrying his friend across the ravaged city, from using up what little strength was left in closing and slumping against the door, too tired now to pull it open, knowing he would have nightmares in the years to come—nightmares of banging on it, wrenching at the handle, calling out to Sándor—only to wake to the terror of loss, alone in the dark with all he'd been separated from, as if there was no way to figure out where he was, where he began and ended, until he realized what was out of reach. It was Sándor's last gift, to József and the lion both, what he thought they needed to live, as if grief could work that way, though in the end it was only what he'd wanted: the death of whatever it was—affection, friendship, love—that kept him in place, reminding him of what he was and in that way of what he'd seen, when all he wanted by then was the roar and the leap—the moment when he was finally something else.

Winter 2010

The Art of the Landscape
SHEROD SANTOS

for Mark Strand

In Sebastião Salgado's photographs
Of Rwandan refugees in Tanzania,
A viewer gets lost momentarily in the epic,
Bosch-like register of death and human suffering,
The far-flung encampments of washpots,
Lean-tos, scattered rags, the emaciated, fly-
Ridden children, the scabbed, hollow-eyed
Men and women gathering twigs, or skewering
Rats for a cook-fire, a populace that appears
To have wandered here across the salt expanse
Of a drought-stricken, uninhabitable earth.
And their suffering is not made less of
Than their suffering is, nor their stares
Made more consolable than we've come
To expect from a grief beyond the reach
Of mercy, for everything about them,
We realize, will go on forever and always.

And yet, somehow, in the face of this same
Unspeakable harm, a photographic fact
Distills the air with a gilt precipitate
Apportioned it by a sunrise that has opened up
A thin empyrean of golden light, the strata
Of cloud illumined with some vaulted
Aspect of sublimity such as one might see
In a nineteenth-century landscape painted
By Kensett or Whittredge or Heade,

192 • RARITAN ON WAR

Though the light of those paintings, infused
With an aureate splendor borne of plenitude
And awe, outshines a world composed
In shades of everything except what's human.
And isn't that, after all, what worries us most
About this picture? A beauty unchastened
By experience? The idea that with deliberate care,
With weighed precision, the photographer
Has taken the measure of some pale
Effulgence that falls with what is hardly grace
On the whole anonymous tragedy held
In the hollow of an outstretched hand?
Or is it more that this is a landscape
From which human suffering is not dispelled?
That theirs is a misery before which
The beautiful, however haphazard,
However unwilled, might insusceptibly
Make itself known? That contrary to some line
We've drawn between what we honor
And what deplore, the two might actually
Subsist somewhere within the province
Of each other's worlds?

A rent in memory,
And *Time* recalls another photograph
By a photo-journalist free-lancing shots
Out around the benchlands near Kosovo.
In a small, poppy-filled clearing in the woods
Two hundred meters above the mountain
Village of Velika Krusa, he has stumbled on
A Serbian soldier who, except for certain
Small details, seems poised above the history
He's making, afloat in the ether of a storybook
World where even our fears are transfigured.

SHEROD SANTOS • 193

For within that world the soldier is tensed
And bent to play an English rosewood upright
Piano whose burnished surface is haloed
In the tailings of a winter sun. To the right
Of him, there is stacked up what appears to be
A cache of musical instruments; to the left,
A mounded tarpaulin against which rests
A Russian Dragunov sniper's rifle
With a night scope and box magazine.
There couldn't be more than an hour or so
Of daylight left. And were our visions
Keen enough, we could just make out,
Halfway up the mountainside, the access
To a shallow cave, and within that cave,
Hunkered together against the cold, what
Remains of a family of Albanian musicians
Whose upright piano that soldier plays.

The family—a grandmother and her brother,
A mother with her two daughters and son—
Has sheltered in the cave for eighteen days
On a week's supply of water and bread
And dried sausages. And so it happens
That beyond all sense, rising up through
The chill gradations of the mountain air,
The family hears, or imagines it hears,
The obscure but familiar chords of a Mozart
Concerto in D Minor; and so clearly
Does the music filter up off the valley floor
That they can tell from the luff of a single
Out-of-tune G-flat key that their piano
Is the one being played, and that the person
Who plays it does so with exceptional
Tenderness and care. So much so that all

The while the music plays they find
Themselves inclining nearer the mouth
Of the cave, leaning out into the fleet *andante*
Of each carefully articulated measure.
And for what still seems a moment pitched
Well beyond the reach of space and time,
They take it all in, the thin, collecting overtones,
The loosely modulating lilts and falls,
The trills and tailed *arpeggios*, they take it all in
And hold it there, as if the weight of each note
Could quicken the mind's capacities,
As if the mind could actually abide such things
As a sniper's hands on the piano keys
Of a Mozart Concerto in D Minor.

Summer 2002

CONTRIBUTORS

C. FELIX AMERASINGHE is a Sri Lankan American author who practiced law for fourteen years before leaving the profession in 2015 to write and paint full time. His short stories have been published in *upstreet*, *Salt Hill*, and *Raritan*. He has written a collection of eight short stories that focus on the loneliness of the immigrant experience in the United States and elsewhere in the world, several of which operate in the context of Sri Lanka's brutal ethnic conflict.

ANDREW J. BACEVICH is board chair and co-founder of the Quincy Institute for Responsible Statecraft.

CAI GUO-QIANG was born in Quanzhou, China, and his work crosses multiple mediums within art including drawing, installation, video, and performance. His 2019 solo exhibitions include *In the Volcano* at the National Archaeological Museum of Naples, *The Transient Landscape* at the National Gallery of Victoria, Melbourne, and *Cuyahoga River Lightning* at the Cleveland Museum of Art. He currently lives and works in New York.

VICTORIA DE GRAZIA is Moore Collegiate Professor Emerita of History at Columbia University. Her most recent book is *The Perfect Fascist: A Story of Love, Power, and Morality in Mussolini's Italy*.

TAMAS DOBOZY, a professor in the Department of English and Film Studies at Wilfrid Laurier University, lives in Kitchener, Ontario, Canada. He has published four books of short fiction. One, *Siege 13*, won the 2012 Rogers Writers Trust of Canada Fiction Prize, and was shortlisted for both the Governor General's Award: Fiction and the 2013 Frank O'Connor International Short Story Award. Dobozy has published over eighty short stories in journals such as *One Story*, *Fiction*, *Agni*, and *Granta*, and his scholarly work—on music, utopianism, American literature, the short story, and poststructuralism—

CONTRIBUTORS • 197

has appeared in *Canadian Literature*, *Genre*, *Modern Fiction Studies*, and elsewhere.

DAVID FERRY (1924–2023) was a poet, translator, and Sophie Chantal Hart Professor Emeritus of English at Wellesley College. He published many notable translations, including *Gilgamesh: A New Rendering in English Verse*, the *Georgics*, *Eclogues*, and *Aeneid* of Virgil, and the *Epistles* and *Odes* of Horace, as well as several volumes of poetry, including *Bewilderment: New Poems and Translations* (winner of the National Book Award in 2012) and *Of No Country I Know: New and Selected Poems and Translations* (winner of the Lenore Marshall Poetry Prize in 2000).

M. FORTUNA lives and works in the Delaware Valley. *Percussion of Cut and Salve* is part of a series, *Swansquarter: The Wound-Dresser's Dreaming*, shown at the Institute for Advanced Studies in Culture at the University of Virginia.

EMMA DODGE HANSON'S books include *Solo: Women Singer-Songwriters* and *Faces of Layla*. Her most recent work supports Drilling for Hope (drillingforhope.org), a nonprofit that brings clean water to communities in the developing world.

JOCHEN HELLBECK is Distinguished Professor of History at Rutgers University and the author of *Stalingrad: The City that Defeated the Third Reich* and, most recently, *"World Enemy No. 1": Nazi Germany, the Soviet Union, and the Jews*, to be published by Penguin Press in Fall 2025.

KARL KIRCHWEY is the author of seven books of poems. He teaches in the MFA Program in Creative Writing at Boston University. "Halberstadt" is part of a long-poem-in-progress called *Mutabor*. He is also the author of a cycle of seven linked hybrid essays called *Grim Reapers: A Family History of Ambiguous Loss* concerning his uncle, a naval aviator lost in the Pacific in World War II. One of these essays, "Hope Till Hope Creates," appeared in the spring 2023 issue of *Raritan*.

198 • RARITAN ON WAR

RAY KLIMEK is a visual artist and writer who lives in Highland Park, New Jersey. *Remote Viewing*, his video collaboration with the poet Judson Evans, was recently selected by the Athens International Film and Video Festival in Ohio. Work from his long-term project, *Carbon*, has been widely exhibited and was the subject of a one-person show at the Sordoni Gallery in Wilkes-Barre, Pennsylvania. His work can be seen at rayklimek.com.

PETER LABIER is an interdisciplinary artist working in painting, drawing, music, dance, and performance. He is the founding member of the New York-based band Psychobuildings. LaBier's work has been exhibited in New York, Los Angeles, Miami, Houston, Berlin, and Hamburg. LaBier received his BA at Vassar College and his MFA from Columbia University.

PATRICK LAWRENCE was a correspondent abroad for many years, chiefly for the *International Herald Tribune*. He now writes foreign affairs commentary for *Consortium News*, *ScheerPost*, and *Current Concerns*, *Horizons et débats*, and *Zeit-Fragen*. His most recent books are *Time No Longer: Americans after the American Century* and *Journalists and Their Shadows*.

DAVID MARK LEVITT (d. mark levitt) hails from Athens, Georgia, and is a self-described unaffiliated skeptic, beatnik, peacenik, animal lover, and Thelonious Monk fan.

MICHAEL MILLER'S poem "The Different War" was the 2014 first-prize winner of the W. B. Yeats Society Poetry Award; other war poems have appeared in the *Sewanee Review*, *Raritan*, *Commonweal*, and elsewhere. His third book, *Darkening the Grass*, was a Massachusetts Book Award "Must-Read" selection for 2013. His new book, *War Zone*, is forthcoming from Citizen Line Books. Born in 1940, Miller served four years in the United States Marine Corps.

LYLE JEREMY RUBIN is the author of *Pain Is Weakness Leaving the Body: A Marine's Unbecoming*.

CONTRIBUTORS · 199

ELIZABETH D. SAMET is a professor of English at West Point. Her most recent book is *Looking for the Good War: American Amnesia and the Violent Pursuit of Happiness*, which won the American Philosophical Society's Jacques Barzun Prize in Cultural History. The opinions expressed in "Make Movies, Not War" do not reflect the official policy or position of the Department of the Army, the Department of Defense, or the U.S. government.

SHEROD SANTOS is a poet, playwright, and translator. He lives in Santa Fe and works for a hunger outreach program in northern New Mexico. His newest collection of poems is *The Burning World*.

ROBERT WESTBROOK is Joseph F. Cunningham Professor Emeritus of History at the University of Rochester. His books include *John Dewey and American Democracy*, *Why We Fought*, and *Democratic Hope*. He has been a *Raritan* contributor since 2007.

ABOUT THE EDITORS

JACKSON LEARS is Board of Governors Distinguished Professor of History at Rutgers University and editor in chief of *Raritan Quarterly*. He has written five books in American cultural history, the most recent of which is *Animal Spirits: The American Pursuit of Vitality from Camp Meeting to Wall Street*. His essays and reviews have appeared in the *London Review of Books*, *The New York Review of Books*, *The Nation*, and *The New Republic*; they have been collected in *Conjurers, Cranks, Provincials, and Antediluvians: The Off-Modern in American History*.

KAREN PARKER LEARS is associate editor of *Raritan Quarterly*. From her art studio, Swansquarter, she works under the name M. Fortuna. She has had solo shows at Princeton University, the Institute for Advanced Studies in Culture at the University of Virginia, and the Johnson & Johnson World Headquarters Gallery in New Brunswick, New Jersey. She created illuminations for *Women Writers of Latin America: Intimate Histories*. Her work can be viewed at swansquarter.com.

IMAGE CREDITS

PAGE 11: Map by Cassandra Nozil. Reproduced with permission.

PAGE 14: Photograph by S. Loskutov. Courtesy of Jochen Hellbeck.

PAGE 18: Photograph by Georgy Samsonov. Courtesy of Jochen Hellbeck.

PAGE 21: Photograph by N. Sitnikov. Courtesy of Jochen Hellbeck.

PAGE 28: Photograph by shinobi / Shutterstock.com.

PAGE 91: © M. Fortuna. Reproduced with permission.

PAGE 93: © Peter LaBier. Reproduced with permission.

PAGE 95: © Ray Klimek. Reproduced with permission.

PAGE 97: © d. mark levitt. Reproduced with permission.

PAGE 99: The Museum of Modern Art, New York. Gift of Clarissa Alcock Bronfman. © Cai Guo-Qiang. Digital image © The Museum of Modern Art. Licensed by Scala / Art Resource, New York. Reproduced with permission from Cai Studio, New York.

PAGES 104–113: © Emma Dodge Hanson. Reproduced with permission.

PAGE 143: Photograph courtesy of Karl Kirchwey.

PAGE 144: Photograph courtesy of Karl Kirchwey.

PAGE 146: Photograph (#fo3025) courtesy Städtisches Museum Halberstadt.

PAGE 149: Photograph (#fo3062 a-g) courtesy Städtisches Museum Halberstadt.

PAGE 151: Photographs courtesy of Karl Kirchwey.

PERMISSIONS

"The Animals of the Budapest Zoo, 1944–1945" by Tamas Dobozy is from *Raritan* (Summer 2010) and was later revised by the author and published in their collection *Siege 13*. Copyright © 2010 by Tamas Dobozy. Reprinted with the permission of The Permissions Company, LLC, on behalf of Milkweed Editions (milkweed.org).

The excerpt from the *Aeneid* used with permission of the University of Chicago Press Books, from *The Aeneid* by Virgil, translated by David Ferry. Copyright © 2017; permission conveyed through Copyright Clearance Center, Inc.

"The Art of the Landscape" by Sherod Santos is from his collection *The Perishing*. Copyright © 2003 by Sherod Santos. Used by permission of W. W. Norton & Company, Inc.

INDEX

Abu Ghraib prison (Iraq), torture scandal at, 41, 49, 79, 85, 120; Bourne's warning on "war-technique" and, 163; government response to, 81; perpetrators from U.S. Army, 83; public breaking of scandal, 80

Adler, Renata, 84–84

Aeneid (Virgil), ix, 87–88

Afghanistan, American war in, 34, 119, 121, 122, 174

Agamben, Giorgio, 48, 50

Agee, James, 122

Aideed, Mohamed Farah, 80

Air Force, U.S., 143, 174

airpower, 118

Ai Weiwei, 37

Alexievich, Svetlana, 5, 23, 27, 30

Algiers (film, 1938), 134

Ali, Tariq, 37

Al Jazeera, 55, 120, 121

Anaconda, Operation, 119

antifascism: General Paulus and, 112; Stalingrad's centrality to myth of, 26

anti-Semitism, 162

Arab-Israeli War (1973), 175

Arendt, Hannah, 46–47, 50

Armenian genocide, 25

Army, U.S., 34, 118

Arrow Cross (Hungarian fascists), 177, 178, 184

Assange, Julian, ix, 175; as archetype, 55, 56; arrest of (2019), 32, 33, 49; character assassination campaign against, 51–52; court appearances, 42–46; "culture of secrecy" combated by, 37–38; defense strategy of, 41–42; In Ecuadorian Embassy (London), 32, 36, 37, 39; legal campaigns against, 35–36; as object of purification ritual, 54; public images of, 32–33; U.S. extradition request for, 34, 36; whistle-blowing and, 41; work with Chelsea Manning, 35, 36, 38

Auschwitz, 26

authenticity, cinema and, 125, 129, 131, 135, 138

Avila, Renata, 53

Baraitser, Judge Vanessa, 43, 44, 45, 46, 49; claim to sovereign preroga-tive, 50–51; corruptions of due process by, 50

Battle of Algiers, The (film, dir. Pontecorvo, 1966): "anti-art" style in, 131; Criterion Collection package, 128; critical responses to, 132, 134–135; disjuncture between image and political context, 137; between documentary and fiction, 135–136; musical score of, 131–132; nonprofessional actors in, 133–134; Pentagon screening of (2003), 126–127; representation of reality of war and, 129; resurrection of, 127. *See also* Pontecorvo, Gillo

205

206 • INDEX

Beck, Ulrich, 161

Belmarsh prison (London), ix, 32, 39, 41, 42; Assange's circumstances at, 44–45; totalitarian experiment at, 48

Benjamin, Walter, 146

Ben M'Hidi, Larbi, 136–137

Berlin standoff (1961), 171

Berman, Paul, 161, 162

Bernhardt, Sarah, 136

Bin Laden, Osama, 120

Binney, Bill, 41

Birth of a Nation (film, dir. Griffith, 1915), 137

Bitburg cemetery (Germany), 24–25

Black Hawk Down (Bowden, 1999), 119

Black Panthers, 126

Blair, Tony, 82

Bonfiglio, Dominic, 5

Boufflers, Maréchal de, 115

Bourgogne, Duc de, 115

Bourne, Randolph, ix, 156, 167, 168, 169; on consequences of "war-technique," 163; criticism of pro-war liberals, 156, 157, 159, 162; as forgotten figure, 157; "realistic pacifism" and, 157–158; as supporter of "armed neutrality," 166; on war as "health of the state," 156, 165

Bowden, Mark, 119

Brady, Mathew, 120–121, 125

Brecht, Bertolt, 12

Bresson, Robert, 134

Budapest Zoo, animals of, 177–179; elusive lion of, 181, 185–187; frozen to death, 181; harmony of immedi-

ate needs, 184–185; human–lion metamorphosis, 187, 188–190; "liberation" of, 181–183, 185; life and death of keepers, 179–181; slaughtered by starving citizens, 179

Bulletin of the Atomic Scientists, 171

bureaucracy, viii, ix, 81

Burke, Edmund, 123

Bush, George W., x, 76–77, 78, 80; compared to Woodrow Wilson, 157; congressional authorization to go to war, 86; decision to wage war on Iraq, 82; justification for Iraq War, 160

Bush Doctrine, 165

Butler, Samuel, 127

Cabinet of Dr. Caligari, The (film, 1920), 138

Cai Guo-Qiang, 98

Cambodia, 174

Canaries in the Mineshaft: Essays on Politics and Media (Adler), 84

capitalism, 20

Capra, Frank, 129

Carbon Burn (Klimek, 2015), 94, 95

Carter, Jimmy, 23

Catch-22 (Heller), vii–viii

Chekhov, Anatoly, 19–20

Cheney, Dick, 162

Chernobyl nuclear power plant, 170

Chile, 174

China, as nuclear power, 170, 172

Chomsky, Noam, 46, 156

Christian Democratic Party (Germany), 24

Chuikov, Lieutenant General Vassiliy, 16–17, 102, *105*, 106–107

INDEX • 207

Churchill, Winston, 22
CIA (Central Intelligence Agency), ix, 44, 52, 78, 176
cinema, war and, 125–139
Cipher Bureau, 41
Civil War, American, 117, 120–121, 125
Clancarty, Earl of, 117
Clarke, Richard A., 127, 128
Clurman, Harold, 128, 134–135
Cockburn, Patrick, 53
Cold War, ix–x, 6, 7, 15, 23, 80; cult of imperial presidency and, 76; nuclear war threat and, 170
"Collapse of American Strategy, The" (Bourne, 1917), 157
Collective Autobiographyt of the Soviet People during the Civil War (Gorky and Mints), 19
Come and See (film, dir. Klimov, 1985), 5–6
Compiègne, staged battle at (1698), 115–116, 138
Comprehensive Nuclear Test Ban Treaty, 176
Congress, US, ix, 77
Control Room (documentary film, dir. Noujaim, 2004), 121–122
Crimea, Russian annexation of (2014), 27
CSIS (Center for Strategic and International Studies), 52
Cuban missile crisis, 175

Dachau, liberation of, 4
Danner, Mark, 76, 76, 78, 81
Dearlove, Sir Richard, 83
Deep Throat, of Watergate scandal, 41

de Grazia, Captain A. J., Jr., 30
democracy, 6, 38, 76, 85–86; fostered at gunpoint, 167; national security and, 85; resurrected meaning of, xi; war and, ix, 157, 161; Wilsonian liberalism and, 162
Desert Storm, Operation, 80, 83
Dewey, John, 156, 157, 158, 161, 162; betrayal of pragmatism in World War I, 167; on militarist conception of noble war, 163
Dimmack, Gordon, 41, 48
disinformation, 9, 34, 35, 77
Dr. Strangelove (film, dir. Kubrick, 1964), 172
Doomsday Machine, The: Confessions of a Nuclear War Planner (Ellsberg), 170, 175
Dos Passos, John, 156
Douhet, Giulio, 174
Drake, Tom, 41
Drawing for a Transient Rainbow (Cai Guo-Qiang, 2003), 98, 99
Drif-Bitat, Zohra, 133
Duka, A. S. (Red Army soldier), 18
Duvivier, Julien, 133

Ecuador, 34
Eisenhower, Dwight D., 173
Ellsberg, Daniel, 40–41, 53, 175–176; on military assaults against civilians, 173–174; on threat of nuclear war, 170–173, 175. *See also* Pentagon Papers
Enduring Freedom, Operation, 80
England, Lyndie, 81
Eremenko, General Andrei, 107
Espionage Act (1917), 36

208 • INDEX

European Union, 6, 7, 27, 30
Evans, Walker, 122

Fable of the Bees, The (Mandeville, 1714), 124
fascism, 4, 26
FBI (Federal Bureau of Investigation), 41
Felt, Mark, 41
FLN [National Liberation Front] (Algeriia), 132, 135, 136
"fog of war," x
For a Few Dollars More (film, dir. Leone, 1965), 131
Ford, John, 129
Fortuna, M., 90
France, 4, 12, 30, 62, 170
French New Wave cinema, 126, 137
Freund, Charles Paul, 127, 135
Fukushima Daiichi nuclear power plant, 170
Fuller, Samuel, 138
funeral pyres, for fallen soldiers, 87–88
Fussell, Paul, vii, 129

Gabin, Jean, 134
Garrison General William F., 118–119
Gauck, Joachim, 29
Gaza war, x
Geneva Convention, 81
genocide, 6, 25, 164, 174
German Historical Institute of Moscow, 8
Germany, Federal Republic of, 23, 24, 27, 29
Girard, René, 53, 54
glasnost, 6, 23

"Global War on Terror," 76
Godard, Jean-Luc, 137, 138
god is water (levitt, 1998), 96, 97
Goebbels, Joseph, 10
Gorbachev, Mikhail, 23
Göring, Hermann, 4
Gorky, Maxim, 19
Grant, Ulysses S., 117, 118
Great Depression, 76
Great War and Modern Memory, The (Fussell), vii
Griffith, D. W., 137
Grossman, Vassily, 5, 20, 22, 25–26, 106. See also Life and Fate
Guantánamo Bay captives, 39, 49
Guatemala, 174
Guernica, bombing of, 174
Gulf of Mexico oil spill, 170

Habermas, Jürgen, 25
Halberstadt, bombing of, ix, 140, 141, 145–146; aftermath of bombing (photograph), 146; American airmen involved in, 148, 151, 150; B-17 Flying Fortress (Cohen drawing, 1945), 144; film documentation of, 150–151; Hungarian refugees in Halberstadt, 141–142; survivors of, 147, 149, 148, 152; U.S. Army Air Force map of Halberstadt, 143
Hamilton, Rita, 116
Hellbeck, Jochen, 5, 8, 12, 15; family history and Stalingrad, 22–23; on German remembrance of Stalingrad, 25–26
Heller, Joseph, vii
Hemingway, Ernest, ix, xi

INDEX · 209

Hetherington, Tim, 122

Hindenlang, Gerhard, 102–103, 109, *110–113*, 111–112, 114

Hiroshima, atomic bombing of, 171

Hitchens, Christopher, 161, 162

Hitler, Adolf, 9, 22, 101; Operation Barbarossa, 25; Paulus promoted to Field Marshal by, 10, 109

Hollywood cinema, 121, 125–126, 130, 134, 137

Holocaust, 6, 7; intensified by German defeat at Stalingrad, 10; relation to war in Eastern Front, 29–30

Homo Sacer (Agamben), 48

Hoon, Geoffrey, 83

human rights, 86, 161, 162, 164–165

Human Rights Watch, 164

Hussein, Saddam, 80, 82; chemical weapons used by, 164; falling statue of, 163; overthrow of, 161; WMD (weapons of mass destruction) and, 83, 160

Huston, John, 129

hydrogen bomb, 171

Ignatieff, Michael, 120, 161, 162, 163, 167

Ignatius, David, 126

Imaginary Signifier, The (Metz, 1977), 136

imperialism, 162, 165, 167

In Defense of Julian Assange (Ali and Kunstler, eds.), 37, 42, 46, 52, 53, 54

Independent Panel to Review Department of Defense Detention Operations, 81

India, 170

Institute of Russian History (Russian Academy of Sciences), 8

Iran, 172, 174, 176

Iraqi Freedom, Operation, 80

Iraq War, 73, 76, 80, 121, 123, 174; Downing Street memo and, 82–85; as human rights disaster, 164–165, 167; Iraqi self-determination and, 168–169; media perspectives on, 120; No-Fly Zones, 83; Pentagon screening of *The Battle of Algiers*, 126; pertinence of Bourne's war essays to, 157–158, 168; Wilsonian justifications for, 157

Israel: erasure of Palestinian presence by, x; as nuclear power, 170

ISSO (Information Security Oversight Office), 37

James, William, 167

Johnson, Lyndon B., 174

Johnstone, Caitlin, 52

Jones-Fay Report, 80

journalism, 77, 119; "balanced," 83–84; Battle of Stalingrad and, 20; complicity in "Age of Frozen Scandal," 82; cynicism and, 84; fraud perpetrated by, 85; photo-journalism, 125, 192; politics as usual and, 78; WikiLeaks and, 38, 55–56

Junger, Sebastian, 122

Just Cause, Operation, 80

just war theory, 166

Kaminski, Janusz, 129

Kaplan, Lawrence, 161

Katrine, Hurricane, 78, 170

210 • INDEX

Kaufman, Michael T., 126
Kazak Red Army troops, 13
Keegan, John, 117–118
Kennedy, John F., 174
Khruschchev. Nikita, 15
Kipling, Rudyard, vii
Kirchwey, George W., *151*
Kissinger, Henry, 175
Klawans, Stuart, 132
Klimek, Ray, 94
Klimov, Elem, 5, 6
Kluge, Alexander, 153
Kohl, Helmut, 24, 25
Korea, North, 171, 172, 176
Korean War, 174
Koshkarev, A. F., 17
Kosovo, 165, 192–194
Kracauer, Siegfried, 130
Kristol, William, 161
Kunstler, Margaret, 37

Labier, Peter, 92
landscape, human suffering and, 191–194
language: abstractions of bureaucracy and, viii; limits of, vii
Laos, 174
Lasch, Christopher, 156
Latvian Red Army troops, 13
Laurence, John, 125
law, international, 165
learned helplessness, 43, 46, 47
Lee, Spike, 128
Lehar, Franz, 101
LeMay, General Curtis, 174
Leone, Sergio, 131
levitt, d. mark, 96
Lewis, James, 44

Libby, Scooter, 78–79
Libya, 174
Life and Fate (Grossman, 1960), 5, 22, 25–26, 107
Loomis, Ed, 41
Louis XIV, staged battle at Compiègene, 115–116, 138
"Love Song to Stalingrad, A" (Neruda, 1942), 12
Lynch, Jessica, 80

Macdonald, Dwight, 156
Mahadevabalasingham, Arunachalam (aka Bob): adoption of new name, 65; chess as significant interest of, 59, 62, 64–65, 68–69, 75; education in America, 63–64; encounter with art therapist, 65–66; escape from Sri Lanka, 62–63; experience of Sri Lankan civil war, 59–62; false identity in America, 68; memories of war, 64; at school graduation ceremony, 70–75
Maintenon, Madame de, 115, 116
Mandeville, Bernard, 124
Man Escaped, A (film, dir. Bresson, 1956), 134
Manning, Chelsea, 35, 36, 38, 175; "Gitmo Files" and, 39; imprisonment of, 39–40, 49
Mao Tse-tung, 10
Marshall, General George, 174
Martin, Jean, 132
Mask of Command, The (Keegan, 1987), 117
Maurizi, Stefania, 53
media, mainstream, x, 52, 55–57

INDEX • 211

Melzer, Nils, 35–36, 42
Méndez, Juan, 39
Merezhko, Anatoly Grigorevich, 102–108, *104, 105, 106, 107*
Merkel, Angela, 27, 29
Metz, Christian, 135, 136
Mexican War, 117
MI6 (British foreign intelligence branch), 82, 83
"military humanism," 161–162, 166–167
Miller, Judith, 85
Miller, Michael, 58
Milošević, Slobodan, 80
Mints, Isaak, 18–19, 22
misinformation, 35
Mogadishu raid (1993), 119
Morricone, Ennio, 131
Motherland Calls, The (statue), 15, 28
Moynihan, Daniel Patrick, 37
Murray, Craig, 42–45, 47, 49
music, in wartime, 193–194
Mussolini, Benito, 27, 174

Nagasaki, atomic bombing of, 171
nationalism: German, 25; Russian, 29
national security, ix, 38, 51, 170
NATO (North Atlantic Treaty Organization), x, 7, 25, 30, 175
Nazism, 3, 4, 20, 46, 177, 184; debate in postwar Federal Germany over reckoning with, 24–25; European Axis allies of, 10; New Order, 6, 8, 26–27; race war against "Judeo-Bolshevism," 6, 10, 30
neoconservatives, 161
neorealist cinema, Italian, 126, 130
Neruda, Pablo, 12

New START (New Strategic Arms Reduction Treaty), 172, 176
New York Times, 20, 77, 120, 126, 176; Iraq War and, 55–56, 85; Pentagon Papers and, 41
Niebuhr, Reinhold, 165
9/11 (September 11, 2001, terrorist attacks), 76, 78, 128
1919 (Dos Passos), 156
Nixon, Richard, 175
NKVD paramilitary units, 15, 16
Nolte, Ernst, 25
Noriega, Manuel, 80
Norton, Lucy, 115
Noujaim, Jehane, 121
NSA (National Security Agency), 40, 41
nuclear war, threat of, 23, 170–173, 175
nuclear winter, 171

Obama, Barack, 35, 39
Origins of Totalitarianism, The (Arendt), 46–47

Pahl, Jon, 49
Paisan (film, dir. Rossellini, 1946), 130
Pakistan, 171
Palestine Liberation Organization, 126
Palestine/Palestinians, x, 174
Palin, Sarah, 38
"Past Which Will Not Pass, The" (Nolte), 25
Paulus, Field Marshal Friedrich von, 10, 27, 109, 111–112
Pax Americana, 76

212 • INDEX

Pearl, Daniel, 120
Pentagon Papers, 41, 170, 175
Pépé le Moko (film, dir. Duvivier, 1937), 133, 134
Percussion of Cut and Salve (Fortuna, 2007), 90, *91*
perestroika, 6
Perle, Richard, 161
Perry, Janet, 116
Pevear. Richard, 5
photography, war and: in *The Battle of Algiers*, 132; Brady's photographs of Antietam, 120–121, 125; moral sense and, 124–125
Pilger, John, 53
Poem of the Cid, 116
Pompeo, Mike, 52
Pontecorvo, Gillo, 126, 127, 129, 131; cast of actors and nonactors, 133; "dictatorship of truth" aesthetic, 132–133, 137, 138. See also *Battle of Algiers, The*
Popular Front, 4, 26
Potsdam agreement (1945), 7
Predator drones, 118
Provance, Samuel, 41
Putin, Vladimir, 27, 172

al-Qaeda, 120, 128, 160

Reagan, Ronald, 23–24, 79
Red Army, Soviet: Budapest captured by (1944–45), 177, 178, 182, 185, 188; German attitude toward, 13; non-Russian nationalities in, 13; political commissars in, 17–18; Sixty-Second Army, 101, 106; "swapping without looking"

tradition, 107–108; Western historians' misrepresentation of, 15. *See also* Stalingrad
refugees: Hungarians in Halberstadt, 141–142; Rwandans in Tanzania, 191; from Sri Lankan civil war, 62–63; of Stalingrad, 9, *21*
Regarding the Pain of Others (Sontag, 2003), 123, 124–125
Restrepo (film, dir. Scranton, 2010), 122
Rieff, David, 167
Rodimtsev, General, 16
Rome, Open City (film, dir. Rossellini, 1945), 130–131, 132, 137
Roosevelt, Franklin D., 22, 174
Roske, Colonel Friedrich, 109, 111–112, *111*
Rossellini, Roberto, 130–131, 137
Roth, Kenneth, 164–165
Rousseau, Jean-Jacques, 124
Rove, Karl, 162
rule of law, 85, 86
Rumsfeld, Dondald, 81, 162
Russia, post-Soviet, 27, 52; memory of Stalingrad in, 102, 103; NATO expansion and, 7; nuclear arms race and, 172; as nuclear power, 172; proxy war against, x; Russian Federation, 6
"Russiagate," 52
Russian Commission on the History of the Great Patriotic War, 5, 8

Saint-Simon, Duc de, 115, 116
Salem with trials, 54
Salgado, Sebastião, 191
Sanders, Bernie, 176

INDEX · 213

Sands of Iwo Jima (film, dir. Ford, 1949), 129
Saudi Arabia, 174
Saving Private Ryan (film, dir. Spielberg, 1998), 129, 130
Schlesinger Report, 80
Schnabel, Julian, 128
school shootings, fantasy and reality of, 73, 74
Scott, A. O., 130
Scranton, Deborah, 122–123
secrecy, culture of, ix, 37–38, 40, 53
Secret Way to War, The (Danner), 76, 77, 82
Seven Arts, The (journal), 156
Sheehan, Michael A., 127
Sherman, General William T., 174
show trials, 34
Shtrum, Viktor, 26
silence, viii, 55; of Assange, 33; valor of, vii
Sinhalese language, 61, 63
Sixth Army, Wehrmacht, 9, 10, 101, 109; monument to, 114; surrender of, 27; urban warfare as "Rat Warfare" (*Rattenskrieg*), 17. *See also* Stalingrad
Six Years from Afghanistan (Miller, 2018), 58
slavery, 49
slogans, vii
Smith, Adam, 123–124
Snowden, Edward, 39, 175
Solinas, Franco, 132
Somme, Battle of the, vii
Sontag, Susan, 123, 124–125, 131
Soviet Union/Soviet Russia, 158, 171, 173, 176; dissolution of, 6, 23, 27;

German Non-Aggression Treaty with, 9, 10; losses in World War II, 4; New Man, 19; Reagan's renewed Cold War and, 23–24; seen as Evil Empire, 8
Speak Up for Assange, 51
Spielberg, Steven, 129
Sri Lanka, cvil war in, 67; child conscription by Tamil Tigers, 59, 60, 69; plight of civilians, 60–61; refugee's international journey, 62–63; surrender of Tamil Tigers, 61; Tamil ghost towns, ix, 60
Stalin, Joseph, 9, 13, 15, 18, 101, 107; Great Purges of, 19, 25; "Not One Step Back" order, 15–16; postwar anticosmopolitan campaign, 22
Stalingrad, ix, *14*; American soldier's gratitude to Soviets, 3, 4, 30; Axis advances, *11*, 101; civilian deaths in, 12–13; commemorated in today's world, 26–31; death toll from, 9; evolution into urban people's war, 16; German surrender, 3, 101–102, 111; Mamayev Kurgan Memorial, 27, 28, 30; Operation Winter Storm, 10; postwar place names in honor of Stalingrad, 12; postwar renaming to Volgograd, 15, 27; refugees' return after the battle, *21*; Soviet encircling operation, 101; symbolic importance in World War II, 9–10; as symbol of antifascism, 4–5; testimonies of German soldiers, 20, 102–103, 109, 111–112, 114; testimonies of Russian/Soviet soldiers, 18–20, 102–108; as turning

214 • INDEX

Stalingrad (cont.)
point of World War II, 102; urban
combat, 16–18, *18*. *See also* Red
Army; Sixth Army, Wehrmacht
Stalingrad Protokolle, Die [*The
Stalingrad Protocols*] (Hellbeck), 22
*Stalingrad: The City That Defeated
the Third Reich* (Hellbeck), 5, 8
Stalinism, 46
Star Wars initiative, 23
"state of exception," 50
Steel, Ronald, 160–161
Steinmeier, Walter, 27
Stevens, George, 129
Stone, Oliver, 128
Stratfor company, 35, 36
Straw, Jack, 82
Sweden, rape charges against
Assange in, 34, 35–36, 39
sympathy, 123–125

Taguba Report, 80
Taibbi, Matt, 53
Tamil language, 68
Tamil Tigers: child conscription by,
59, 60, 69; executions of civilians
carried out by, 59; surrender to Sri
Lankan government forces, 61
Tatar Red Army troops, 13
Tauchen, Christopher, 5
Taylor, Zachary, 117
technology, warfare and, 118, 121
Teleki, Oszkár, 177–178, 180, 182
television, 120
terror, war on, x, 76, 86
Theory of Moral Sentiments, The
(Smith, 1759), 123–124
Thomson, David, 124, 127

torture, 39, 42, 43; in *The Battle
of Algiers*, 134; carried out by
Saddam Hussein regime, 163;
CIA's secret torture sites, 49; Iraq
War and, 78
*Torture and Truth: America, Abu
Ghraib and the War on Terror*
(Danner, 2004), 78, 80
totalitarianism, 26, 47, 49
Treblinka, 26
Truffaut, François, 137
Truman, Harry S., 40, 174
Trump, Donald, 52, 171–172
Tsarevitch, The (Lehar operetta), 101

UC Global company, 44
Ukraine war, x
United Kingdom (UK), 34; Assange's
asylum in Ecuadorian embassy
(London), 36, 37, 39; decision to
wage war on Iraq, 82–83; as nuclear
power, 170
United Nations (UN), 82, 83, 164,
166
United States, x, 30; American
exceptionalism, 162, 167; democracy in, 76; military intervention in
name of human rights, 164; renewal
of Cold War after détente, 23;
reputation of U.S. Armed Forces in
public opinion, 79–80; "supermax"
prisons in, 49; war aims in World
War I, 157–158
*Unwomanly Face of War, The: An
Oral; History of Women in World
War II* (Alexievich, 1985), 5, 23
Ut, Nick, 125
Uzbek Red Army troops, 13, 16, 27

INDEX • **215**

Valerie Plame Affair, 78, 79
video intelligence, 118
Vietnam War, 120, 122, 156, 174; analogy wth *Battle of Algiers*, 128; impact of photojournalism, 125; US threat of nuclear strike in, 175
Vindman, Lieutenant Colonel Alexander, 176
Volokhonsky, Larissa, 5
Vonnegut, Kurt, viii

Walzer, Michael, 166
War Depatment, renaming of, ix
War Tapes, The (documentary film, 2006), 122
Watergate scandal, 41
Waterloo, Battle of, 117
Wellington, Duke of, 117, 118, 125
whistle-blowing, 40–41
White Fright (Labier painting, 2017), 92, 93
Whitman, Walt, viii
Wiebe, Kirk, 41
WikiLeaks, 32, 38, 42, 56; "Afghan War Diary" (July 2010), 34; "Cablegate" (November 2010), 34, 35; "Collateral Murder" video (April 2010), 34; founding of (2006), 51; "Gitmo Files" (April 2011), 39; "The Global Intelligence Files" (2012), 35; "Iraq War Logs" (October 2010), 34, 35, 51, 52, 55, 56; working principles of, 53
Wilson, Woodrow, ix, 156, 158, 160–161
Wilsonians, left, 158, 161–167

Wilsonians, right, 161–165, 167
Wolfowitz, Paul, 160, 161
"Worker Reads History, The" (Brecht), 12
World War I, ix, 16, 118; "armed neutrality" and, 166; Battle of Verdun, 9; Bourne's opposition to, 156, 167; as catastrophe waiting to happen, 170
World War II, vii, 16, 118, 156; American–British second front, 3–4; American memory of, 8; bombings of German cities, 154; films about, 129–130; firebombing of Dresden, 174; German atrocities against Soviet prisoners of war, 29; Grand Alliance of, 6; as the Great Patriotic War of the Soviet Union, 19, 22, 23; internment camps of, 49; map of Nazi-occupied Europe, *11*; Normandy landings, 4, 23–24; reparations paid by Germany to Russia, 7, 29; seventieth anniversay of war's end, 27; Soviet contribution forgotten in the West, 7–8; Soviet losses in, 4; Wehrmacht involve-ment in atrocities, 25; women in, 5, 7, 13, 27. *See also* Budapest Zoo, animals of; Halberstadt, bombing of; Stalingrad
Wyler, William, 129

Yacef, Saadi, 132, 133–134, 138
Yardley, Herbert, 41

Zaytsev, Vassily, 20
Zelensky, Volodymyr, 176